Parenting: From Surviving to Thriving
Workbook

Parenting: From Surviving to Thriving
Workbook

Building Healthy Families in a Changing World

BASED ON THE BOOK BY

CHARLES R. SWINDOLL

Produced in association with CREATIVE MINISTRIES
Insight for Living

W PUBLISHING GROUP
A Division of Thomas Nelson Publishers
Since 1798

www.wpublishinggroup.com

PARENTING: FROM SURVIVING TO THRIVING
WORKBOOK

Published by W Publishing Group, a division of Thomas Nelson, Inc., Post Office Box 141000, Nashville, Tennessee, 37214.

W Publishing Group books may be purchased in bulk for educational, business, fundraising, or sales promotional use. For information, please email SpecialMarkets@ThomasNelson.com.

Published in association with Yates & Yates, LLP, Attorneys and Counselors, Orange, California.

Editorial Staff: Shady Oaks Studio, Bedford, TX 76022
Cover Design: Tobias' Outerwear for Books
Front Cover Photo: © Master File
ISBN 978-1-4185-141-29
Printed in the United States
06 07 09 10 VG 10 9 8 7 6 5 4 3 2 1

FROM THE BIBLE-TEACHING MINISTRY OF CHARLES R. SWINDOLL

Charles R. Swindoll has devoted his life to the clear, practical teaching and application of God's Word and His grace. A pastor at heart, Chuck has served as senior pastor to congregations in Texas, Massachusetts, and California. He currently pastors Stonebriar Community Church in Frisco, Texas, but Chuck's listening audience extends far beyond a local church body. As a leading program in Christian broadcasting, *Insight for Living* airs in major Christian radio markets around the world, reaching people groups in languages they can understand. Chuck's extensive writing ministry has also served the body of Christ worldwide and his leadership as president and now chancellor of Dallas Theological Seminary has helped prepare and equip a new generation for ministry. Chuck and Cynthia, his partner in life and ministry, have four grown children and ten grandchildren.

Based on the original outlines, charts, and transcripts of Charles R. Swindoll's sermons, the workbook text was developed and written by Mark Gaither, Th.M., Dallas Theological Seminary, Dallas, Texas.

Contextual support material was provided by the Creative Ministries Department of Insight for Living.

Editor in Chief: Cynthia Swindoll, President, Insight for Living
Vice President and Theological Editor: Wayne Stiles, Th.M., D. Min., Dallas Theological Seminary
Director of Creative Ministries: Michael J. Svigel, Th.M., Ph.D. candidate, Dallas Theological Seminary
Content Editors: Brie Engeler, B.A., University Scholars, Baylor University
    Amy LaFuria Snedaker, B.A., English, Rhodes College

Project Coordinator: Cari Harris, B.A., Journalism, Grand Canyon University

An effort has been made to locate sources and obtain permission where necessary for the quotations used in this book. In the event of any unintentional omission, a modification will gladly be incorporated in future printings.

Contents

A Letter from Chuck

I'll never forget the evening of September 4, 1961. It was the evening after Cynthia had given birth to our first child. As I drove home to our little apartment on the Dallas Seminary campus, I remember thinking how different the world now looked. Young, single men think they're invincible. Young, married men begin to suspect they are not. Young fathers quickly discover how powerless they really are. That night, I shrank before the overwhelming task of parenting that lay ahead of me. Soon after I arrived home, I fell to my knees and begged the Lord, "Please help me know how to be a dad. Cynthia's never been a mom. We don't know what we're doing; so dear Father, please help us!"

The answer to my prayer came quickly. (God loves to answer prayers of utter helplessness.) Cynthia and I turned to Scripture first and began our long journey of discovery. I soon learned that Dr. Howard Hendricks had developed a course called "The Christian Home," which offered perspectives I had never considered. I took that course and it changed everything for us. I began to apply my newly-acquired Hebrew skills to classic parenting passages from the Old Testament. What I learned in that process became the core principles that guided the rearing of our four children. We made mistakes along the way, of course, and our approach was not even near perfect, but we never felt abandoned by the Lord. We merely hoped our children would survive our parenting process, but to our surprise and delight they actually thrived when we were faithful to apply the Lord's principles.

What you hold in your hands is a carefully guided study of the same Scripture passages I first examined in the 1960s. As you work through the lessons, carefully consider each question, scrutinize each portion of God's Word, look for the Lord's directives and declarations, and pray for wisdom as you practically apply what you learn. I'm confident you will discover, as Cynthia and I did, that the truths contained in the Bible are not only timeless and helpful, but they are indispensable for a child to go from *surviving* their formative years to *thriving* as they reach adulthood.

Charles R. Swindoll

How to Use This Workbook

As parents, we often find ourselves suspended between snowcapped mountains of wonder and exhilaration and craggy chasms of self-doubt and desperation. To be sure, parenting is an adventure and—to borrow a slogan from the Peace Corps—it's the "toughest job you'll ever love." What an incredible privilege we have been given! What an opportunity to grow deeper in our relationship with our heavenly Father! Such privilege and opportunity certainly demand more of us than we can give . . . at present. We need help.

The goal of this workbook is simple: to provide you with encouragement, biblical principles, application, and practical insights that will help you discover what God intends for you and your family. It may serve as a tool for personal devotions or as a guide to help families interact with Scripture as it relates to parenting. Leader helps and straightforward outlines also make this an ideal resource for small-group studies and church curriculum.

A brief introduction to its structure will help you get the most from your study.

THE HEART OF THE MATTER highlights the main idea of the lesson and summarizes the corresponding chapter in the *Parenting: From Surviving to Thriving* hardcover book. The lesson itself is composed of three main teaching sections—"You Are Here," "Discovering the Way," and "Starting Your Journey." Take a moment to flip through the first chapter of the workbook and become familiar with these three main sections found in every chapter.

YOU ARE HERE includes an introduction and thought-provoking questions to orient you to the material covered in the chapter. Groups should plan to spend ten to fifteen minutes in this section.

DISCOVERING THE WAY explores the principles of Scripture through observation and interpretation of key passages, demonstrating the relevance of the Bible to modern life. Parallel passages and additional questions supplement the key Scriptures for more in-depth study. The questions in this workbook were based on the New American Standard Bible (1995 update), but you can use whichever Scripture translation you prefer. This section should require twenty to thirty minutes of group time.

 STARTING YOUR JOURNEY focuses on specific, activity-oriented applications to help you put into practice the principles of the lesson in ways that fit your personality, gifts, and level of spiritual maturity. A group should cover this section in about ten to fifteen minutes.

In the workbook's expanded margins, you'll find insightful quotations and helpful notes with suggestions for small-group study. If you're tackling the material on your own, you can skip past the Leader Helps, but if you're leading a time of group discussion, you'll find some of these hints to be invaluable in your preparation to teach each lesson.

USING THE WORKBOOK FOR SMALL-GROUP STUDY

Designed with the small group in mind, the *Parenting: From Surviving to Thriving Workbook* will be most effective when studied by two or more people with a facilitator. The following suggestions are recommended if you're serving as the small-group facilitator.

Preparation. All group members should try to prepare in advance during the week by working through the lessons as described later under "Using the Workbook for Individual Study." As the leader, you should take additional steps to supplement your preparation either by reading the corresponding chapter in the *Parenting: From Surviving to Thriving* hardcover book or listening to the corresponding sermon. Mastery of the material will build your confidence and competence, and approaching the topic from various perspectives will equip you to freely guide small-group discussion.

Discussion Questions. You should feel free to mold the lesson according to the needs of your unique group. At a minimum, however, the group should cover the questions marked by the clock icons in each of the three main sections during your time together. While planning the lesson you will want to mark additional questions you feel will fit the time allotment, needs, and interests of the group. The questions are divided to assist you in your lesson preparation. Note that the questions marked by the clock icon begin a series of *primary,* or core, questions—meant to contribute to a solid understanding of the lesson. The unmarked series of questions are *secondary*—intended to provide a deeper exploration of the topic and corresponding Scripture passages. Encourage your group to dig into the secondary questions on their own.

Flexibility. During group time, after opening in prayer, lead the group through the lesson you planned in advance. Members may want to share their own answers to the questions, contribute their insights, or steer the discussion in a particular direction that fits the needs of the group. Sometimes group members will want to discuss questions you may have left out of the planned lesson. *Be flexible,* but try to stay on schedule so the group has sufficient time for the final section, "Starting Your Journey," where the application of the lesson begins.

Goal. If it's unrealistic to complete a single lesson during a session, consider continuing where you left off in the next session. The goal is not merely to cover material, but to promote in-depth, personal discussion of the biblical text with a view toward personal response and application. To do this, the group will need to both understand the biblical principles and apply them to their lives.

USING THE WORKBOOK AS A COMPANION TO THE SERMON SERIES AND BOOK

For the greatest depth of study, this workbook should be used as a companion to the book by Charles R. Swindoll, *Parenting: From Surviving to Thriving* (Nashville, Tenn.: W Publishing Group, 2006). Each lesson in the workbook corresponds to the same chapter in the book. The workbook can also be used as a companion to Chuck's sermon series *Parenting: From Surviving to Thriving,* available from Insight for Living at www.insight.org.

USING THE WORKBOOK FOR INDIVIDUAL STUDY

The *Parenting: From Surviving to Thriving Workbook* will facilitate your search through the Scriptures for what God has to say about rearing children. Many of the questions are designed for the entire family to answer and share together in order to increase mutual understanding and encourage a common vision for the future. It can be used for individual study. Here's the method we recommend:

Prayer. Begin each lesson with prayer, asking God to teach you through His Word and to open your heart to the self-discovery afforded by the questions and text of the workbook. Any spiritual discipline must be approached with faith in God, who alone can effect spiritual growth in our lives.

Scripture. Have your Bible handy. As you progress through each workbook chapter, you'll be prompted to read relevant sections of Scripture and answer questions related to the topic. You will also want to look up Scriptures noted in parentheses.

Questions. As you encounter the workbook questions, approach them wisely and creatively. Not every question will be applicable to each person all the time. If you can't answer a question, continue on in the lesson. Let the Holy Spirit guide you through the biblical text and its application, using the questions as general guides in your thinking rather than rigid forms to complete.

Features. Throughout the chapters, you'll find several special features designed to add insight or depth to your study. Use these features to enhance your study and deepen your knowledge of Scripture, history, theology, and your family. An explanation of each feature can be found on the next page.

As you complete each lesson, close in prayer, asking God to apply the wisdom and principles to your life by His Holy Spirit. Then trust that God will work out His will for you in His way and that His Word will bear fruit.

Special Workbook Features

Lessons are supplemented with a variety of special features to summarize and clarify teaching points or to provide opportunities for more advanced study. Although they are not essential for understanding and applying the principles in the lesson, they will offer valuable insight as you work through this material.

GETTING TO THE ROOT

While our English versions of the Scriptures are reliable, studying the original languages can often bring to light nuances of the text that are sometimes missed in translation. This feature explores the meaning of the underlying Hebrew or Greek words or phrases in a particular passage, sometimes providing parallel examples to illuminate the meaning of the inspired text.

DIGGING DEEPER

Various passages in Scripture touch on deeper theological questions or confront modern worldviews and philosophies that conflict with a biblical worldview. This feature will help you gain deeper insight into specific theological and practical issues related to the biblical text.

 DOORWAY TO HISTORY

Sometimes the chronological gap separating us from the original author and readers clouds our understanding of a passage of Scripture. This feature will take you back in time to explore the surrounding history, culture, and customs of the biblical world as they relate to the text.

Our prayer is that the biblical principles and applications you glean from this resource will help you begin to cultivate a rich, authentic relationship with each one of the priceless gifts God has entrusted to you . . . your children.

Lesson One

The Best-Kept Secret of Wise Parenting

— Proverbs 22:6; 20:11 —

THE HEART OF THE MATTER

The popular interpretation of "Train up a child in the way he should go" fails to appreciate the rich, practical childrearing advice the verse contains. It doesn't mean parents dictate the correct way, but rather that they observe the child in order to discover his or her unique abilities, temperament, and interests. Then parents should adapt their training to help the child know and become his or her authentic self.

To prepare for this lesson, read Proverbs 22:6; Proverbs 20:11; and chapter 1 in *Parenting: From Surviving to Thriving*.

YOU ARE HERE

Perhaps one of the greatest errors we can make when it comes to childrearing is to train our children exactly as we were trained. After all, our children are different people than we are, having their own unique temperaments, talents, interests, and styles. Furthermore, our parents were not perfect, so some of their methods were most certainly flawed. They did some things well and other things poorly.

Rather than blindly duplicate our parents' methods, we can learn good parenting skills by carefully reflecting upon

Leader Help

By the end of this lesson, group members should know the meaning behind the key words and phrases of Proverbs 22:6, understand the primary responsibility of parents, resolve to observe their children, and adapt their training methods accordingly.

Train up a child in the way he should go, Even when he is old he will not depart from it.
(Proverbs 22:6)

1

how we were reared, allowing the best and worst of our experiences to shape how we train our own children. Our purpose is not to condemn our parents, but to leave behind what didn't work well and to build upon what did. Use the following questions and exercises to examine your upbringing.

Leader Help
The purpose of this exercise is to help mothers and fathers be open to the idea that they can be the parents they wish theirs had been. Using a dry-erase board or a poster board, have the group identify the qualities of an ideal parent. Many of the suggested qualities will be prompted by a significant personal story. Encourage group members to share stories and to explain why the particular quality has such meaning.

 As you consider your best qualities and strongest attributes, what was your parents' greatest positive contribution to your becoming who you are?

Whom do you consider to have had the greatest positive influence on you during childhood?

Describe how he or she related to you and how that shaped your view of yourself and the world.

In your childhood experience, which quality or pattern of childrearing do you consider to have been the most detrimental to your view of yourself and to your ability to be a successful adult?

Which of these statements do you think is most true of your parents?

❏ My parents were evil people who were deliberately negligent or unkind.

❏ My parents wanted the best for me, but they were too broken and ill-equipped to know how to provide much that was positive.

❏ My parents did, on the whole, a very good job rearing me but made some significant mistakes that affect me today.

❏ My parents were the very best, and any failures on their part were so minor that they have had little negative impact on me.

On the whole, I had a healthy, happy childhood. Nevertheless, every home has its challenges . . . I never felt wanted or respected by either of my parents . . . not deeply. I can't remember many times when I was affirmed by them. And I honestly don't think that they ever really knew who I was, which left them ill-equipped to help me know myself.

—*Parenting: From Surviving to Thriving*

How well do you think your parents did at helping you to discover who you are? In what ways did they help you?

In what ways did your parents hinder you or fail to help you from becoming who God made you to be?

What do you wish your parents had done differently?

 Describe how your parents' childrearing methods have influenced yours.

DISCOVERING THE WAY

Train up a child in the way he should go,
Even when he is old he will not depart
from it. (Proverbs 22:6)

This proverb on childrearing has long been taught with a perplexing interpretation that goes something like this: "Rear your children as moral, upright, God-fearing, churchgoing kids. Be sure they carry a Bible to church, attend lots of Sunday school classes, and attend Christian summer camps. Enforce your rules and regulations with consistency. Make sure they learn the Ten Commandments, the Golden Rule, and several key verses of Scripture. Teach them to pray, and be sure they come to a saving knowledge of Jesus Christ. After all, they're eventually going to sow their wild oats. They'll live in rebellion for a while, then, once they've tired of their fling with the wild side of life, they'll eventually come back to the Lord . . . but only if you raised them right!"

This standard interpretation is not helpful, it's not very hopeful, and it is not an accurate understanding of the rich, picturesque language of the original Hebrew. If we take the time to study the terms and how they are put together in this proverb, we will discover a very refreshing, sensible approach to childrearing that offers both hope and practical guidance.

PROVERBS 22:6 . . . THE RIGHT WAY

Proverbs 22:6 contains only eight Hebrew words, each one packing a wealth of illustration and cultural analogy. Let's study each term in detail.

Hebrew is a language of artists and poets. Almost every word has a metaphorical connection to something in the experience of these people. Hebrew poetry, especially, uses allusion and word pictures that convey meaning by analogy, so that a rich tableau of cultural associations stands behind even the simplest sentences.

—*Parenting: From Surviving to Thriving*

Leader Help

After briefly describing each term or phrase, have the men form one group and the women form another. Ask each group to prepare a word picture or a drawing that reflects the Hebrew idea of "train up" using contemporary culture and images. Then have each group present its illustration to the other. Encourage the groups to discuss, critique, and refine the images.

"Train up ..."

The Hebrew word *hanakh* means "to dedicate, or consecrate."[1] It's used only four times in the Old Testament: three times in reference to dedicating a building and once of a child, here. In several Semitic languages, it stems from a term meaning "palate, roof of mouth, jaws, lower part of mouth, lower jaw of horse, mouth, etc."[2] An Arabic verb, a very close cousin to *hanakh*, pictures the custom of a midwife dipping her finger into crushed dates in order to massage the palate and gums of a newborn. This encouraged the baby's sucking instinct so that nursing could begin as soon as possible. The term in languages similar to Hebrew also means "make experienced, submissive, etc. (as one does a horse by a rope in its mouth)."[3]

So in this single Hebrew term translated "train up," we have the mingled ideas of "dedicate," "mouth," and "make experienced." Also included is the picture of a horse's bridle, which subdues the horse for the purpose of directing its natural energies.

"... a child ..."

In each of the following verses, the Hebrew word *na'ar* refers to a child. Note the considerable variety of ages of the people.

Verse	Approximate Age
1 Samuel 4:21	A newborn baby
Exodus 2:6	A three-month-old
1 Samuel 1:22	An infant
1 Samuel 3:1	A young boy

Genesis 21:12	**A 14-year-old**
Genesis 37:2	**A 17-year-old**
Genesis 34:19	**A young man of marriageable age**

". . . in the way he should go . . ."

The whole meaning of the verse turns on this phrase! Many parents emphasize the word *should*, reading, "in the way he *should* go," which they consider to mean *their* way. However, the literal Hebrew reads, "in accordance with *his* way" (the child's), or even more literally, "upon the mouth of his way." (There's "mouth" again, forming a wordplay with *hanakh*.)

The word translated "way" in this verse is *derek*, which means either "road" in the literal sense, or "characteristic manner" in the figurative. For instance, notice how the word is used in Proverbs 30:18–19:

There are three things which are too wonderful for me,
Four which I do not understand:
The *way* of an eagle in the sky,
The *way* of a serpent on a rock,
The *way* of a ship in the middle of the sea,
And the *way* of a man with a maid. (emphasis added)

Each child has a "way," a characteristic manner that distinguishes him or her from all other children, including brothers and sisters. We receive each child from the hand of God, not as a malleable lump of clay to be molded in whatever way we see fit but as a unique, distinctive person with a destiny. We are to honor God's creation of this one-of-a-kind individual by adapting our training to his or her way.

Leader Help

Ask a volunteer to read Proverbs 30:18–19 aloud. Then spend some time discussing how the word "way" is used in each illustration. Does it mean "road," "characteristic manner," or both?

"... when he is old ..."

The Hebrew word translated "old" in Proverbs 22:6 finds inspiration in the image "hair on the chin." The first wisps of hair growing on the chin of a young man show that manhood is not far away. Here the idea of "old" doesn't mean "one foot in the grave"; it means "when he is mature." Hair begins to appear on the face of a young man at about the age of fifteen or sixteen, and we can expect the age of maturity for young women to correspond. In other words, parents should see the positive results of training the young person begins to exercise his or her independence as an adult.

"... will not depart from it"

The Hebrew word translated "depart" means "to turn aside." When a parent helps a child know herself and follow a path, or "way," consistent with her talents, her interests, and her temperament, the child finds herself walking in harmony with God's plan for her. She has no need to rebel. Her contentment keeps her sensitive to the Lord's leading. Why, then, would she want to depart from the way?

We have seen that these few Hebrew words of Proverbs 22:6 are packed with insight. To summarize, a contemporary paraphrase of this verse in New Testament times would look like this:

> Cultivate a thirst, initiate a hunger, create an appetite for spiritual things in the life of a child of any age, as long as he or she is living under your roof, and do it in keeping with the way he or she is made—disciplining evil while affirming and encouraging the good, the artistic, the beautiful.

When the child begins to walk alone, his or her path will be aimed directly toward the Savior, and he or she will continue to walk in God's sovereignty.

STARTING YOUR JOURNEY

Based on our study of Proverbs 22:6, the best-kept secret of wise parenting can be stated this way:

The job of a parent is to help his or her children come to know themselves, grow to like themselves, and find satisfaction in being themselves.

Proverbs 20:11–12 says, "Even a young man is known by his actions, whether his activity is pure and whether it is right. The ear that hears and the eye that sees—the Lord has made them both" (NET). Your child longs to be known intimately by you, and he or she constantly drops clues for you to notice. If we are to adapt our parental training in order to cooperate with God's design of each of our children, we must first know them. And that comes by careful observation, over time.

Given what you have observed about your child, what nonphysical trait stands out the most to you? This could be a talent, a temperament, an interest, a habit, a way of interacting with the world—anything.

Leader Help

Each child is different from his or her parents and from other siblings. Encourage group members to answer these questions about each of their children. Ask participants to share selected insights during group time to ensure that everyone has a chance to share.

How is this trait positive? How can your child use it constructively?

How is this trait negative? How can it have a negative impact on your child?

How might your child use this trait to serve the Lord and benefit others when he or she becomes an adult?

How does this trait challenge you as a parent?

How can you adapt your training to accommodate your child's "way"?

 How is the child different from you? From your spouse?

How might your parenting techniques vary from that of your parents in light of these differences?

What vocations would you imagine to be well suited for your child?

How will you react when your child's interest in something fizzles? What if he or she fails?

Do you allow for differences among your children, even celebrate them, without comparing?

When you help your children know themselves, like themselves, and be themselves, the path that God has prepared for them will become self-evident. His ordained path will be a natural fit for the people they grow to become. As you adapt your childrearing to cooperate with your child's temperament, interests, and abilities, you will likely find that he or she will have no desire to depart from the path—vocational and spiritual—that you help him or her discover.

Lesson Two

Understanding How Your Child Was Made

— Romans 3:9–18; 5:12–19; Psalm 51:5; 58:3; 139:13–16 —

THE HEART OF THE MATTER

God creates every child with a unique set of interests, abilities, and personality traits. Each child bears His image. In this sense, each child is created to be good. Unfortunately, because Adam sinned, each child inherits a corrupt nature that compels him or her to behave selfishly and to choose rebellion over obedience. Consequently, the role of the parent is crucial. If the parent fails to maintain a balanced perspective, the childrearing process will become too negative, lacking encouragement, or too optimistic, overlooking the need for correction.

To prepare for this lesson, read Romans 3:9–18; 5:12–19; Psalm 51:5; 58:3; 139:13–16; and chapter 2 in *Parenting: From Surviving to Thriving.*

YOU ARE HERE

How we approach the task of discipline depends greatly upon how we view our children—each one individually. Our attitude toward them affects how we do the job of parenting, and if our perspective lacks balance, our natural inclinations may do more harm than good.

Leader Help

By the end of this lesson, group members should adopt a balanced view of their children, accepting that every child is created good but is also corrupted by evil from the moment of conception. They should appreciate the crucial role of parental involvement in the form of correction and instruction.

13

As we begin our journey, spend a few moments reflecting on the following questions. Take your time. Be brutally honest with yourself. If you are like most parents, you will find yourself torn between the "right" answer and the authentic answer. The "right" answer rarely offers opportunity for healing and growth. We encourage you to allow the temporary discomfort of the authentic response to lead you to a new, more fulfilling perspective.

Leader Help

The questions in this section examine how group members feel about their children, which can be a tender subject for some. Before you begin the meeting, speak with each person individually to gauge his or her level of comfort with sharing. Keep the information to yourself, but direct the time of discussion accordingly, respecting the privacy of those who are reluctant.

When you interact with your child, the expression on your face reflects your thinking and sends a message. (For example: "I'm so glad to see you!" or "Your shoes are untied again.") Describe what message you think your child sees on your face when your child enters a room.

When you think of your child, which word instinctively and immediately rings true:

❑   Delight   ❑   Trouble

Give this some thought, and then explain why you think you feel this way.

Suppose your child's teacher calls you one evening to inform you that your child has stolen an item from a fellow student. Which of these *best* describes your immediate emotional reaction?

- ❏ There must be some mistake; my child would never do something like that.

- ❏ This doesn't shock me; sometimes kids make foolish choices.

- ❏ This is no big deal; we'll just have my child return the item and be done with it.

- ❏ I am so disappointed; I had hoped my child would be above this kind of behavior.

- ❏ I should have known this would happen; this child has always been difficult.

- ❏ This is another indication that people are corrupt and cannot be trusted—including my child.

Which of the following best describes your attitude toward addressing the situation described above? Choose only one.

- ❏ This is a grave disappointment from which I will have to recover.

- ❏ With my help, this will be a good opportunity for my child to grow.

- ❏ I'm really going to teach my child an unforgettable lesson.

- ❏ I already have so much to do. I wish this would just go away.

Let's face it, we'd rather have our child's love and hugs than to have him or her view us as the enemy—even for a short time. But if we're willing to be "the bad guy" in order to give our child's world order and definition, the result will be a home free of chaos, where everyone can enjoy freedom and love, acceptance and security, purpose, direction, and an authentic basis for a strong self-image.

—Parenting: From Surviving to Thriving

Leader Help

Some group members may have difficulty with the concept of human depravity because our culture teaches that humanity is basically good. It is important to stay focused on the message of Scripture rather than to debate philosophy. Encourage the group to observe the biblical text carefully in this section.

As parents, we quite naturally look upon our children as a reflection of ourselves. Though unique as people, they remind us of who we were, and they hold the potential to become the kind of people we had hoped to be. This may lead us to view our children through either rose-colored or dark glasses, neither of which allows us to see them as they are. If we are to become effective mentors to our young "disciples," we must perceive our children through the crystal-clear lens of Scripture. Our study of several passages will help give us the Lord's perspective on our children.

DISCOVERING THE WAY

The Bible is a remarkable mirror. And when we hold it in front of humanity, the image we see staring back is both beauty and beast, Dr. Jekyll and Mr. Hyde. When we look on the face of a child, especially an innocent newborn, this dual image may be difficult to accept. This becomes equally difficult to believe during the "terrible twos" for an entirely different reason! Nevertheless, Scripture is plain.

Read Romans 3:9–18. According to Romans 3:9, what percentage of the human race is "under sin"? (Some Bible versions use the word *Greeks* to denote Gentiles, or non-Jews.)

According to Romans 3:10–11, what percentage of the human race is righteous, understands spiritual matters, and seeks God?

According to Romans 3:12, what percentage of the human race (past and present) rebels, does evil, and has become useless?

What two powerful images do you find in Romans 3:13 to describe the extent of human depravity?

Do you think Romans 3:10–18 describes the human race as a whole or the potential of each and every individual? Explain your answer. (See also Jeremiah 17:9)

According to Psalm 51:5 and 58:3, from what age is a person corrupted?

 Digging Deeper

Are children really that bad? Psalm 51:5 describes the newborn as sinful from conception. Psalm 58:3–4 says babies are like little venomous snakes. How can an infant be sinful? The debate over human depravity is not new.

In the fourth century AD, a monk named Pelagius proposed the idea that people are born without a sinful nature. "[He] denied that human sin is inherited from Adam. Man, he said, is free to act righteously or sinfully. . . . Adam, indeed, introduced sin into the world, but only by his corrupting example. There is no direct connection between his sin and the moral condition of mankind."[1]

Augustine, a prominent church bishop, challenged Pelagius on his idea, pointing to important passages like Romans 5:17–19. Augustine taught that people are not merely morally neutral but are corrupt as a race and incapable of good unless prompted by God. Some say he went too far in the opposite direction, but Augustine's view has the weight of biblical evidence on its side. Besides, if people are not enslaved by a sinful nature, at least a handful out of the multiple billions of people living should be sinless. But "there is none righteous, not even one" (Romans 3:10).

In AD 431, the ecumenical council at Ephesus condemned Pelagianism, as did every major council of churches and every confession down through the centuries. "No self-respecting Christian theologian would ever want to be known as a Pelagian."[2]

In Psalm 51:5, David said, "In sin my mother conceived me," which some have used to suggest either that David was illegitimate or that the act of conception is sinful. Neither fits well with the context of the psalm in which David admits his own sinfulness, not that of his parents. He declares that he, like all people, was born as a sinful creature. Psalm 58:3 reinforces the truth that all people are born with an evil bent.

 Read Romans 5:12. What brought sin into the world?

Who is the "one man" originally responsible for the inherited disease of sin?

According to Romans 5:17–19, what are three tragic outcomes that still afflict us today?

"By the transgression of the one, . . .
_____" (Romans 5:17).

"Through one transgression there resulted . . .
_____" (Romans 5:18).

"Through the one man's disobedience . . .
_____" (Romans 5:19).

═

Each child was created
by God to be good.
When we look upon a
toddler, what do we typ-
ically see? Spit-up, grass
stains, untied shoelaces,
a bundle of needs, and
constant demands. What
if, instead, we asked,
"What remarkable person
will this one become?"
"What gifts and abilities
will emerge soon?" "How
will this one fit into
God's grand design for
the world?"

—*Parenting: From*
Surviving to Thriving

The Bible makes it clear that every human being has
inherited a sinful nature—even sweet little babies.
Beating in the chest of every child is a strong, selfish will
that wants to be happy and will do almost anything to
please self. The child thinks that by having his own way,
he can avoid painful experiences and sate his desires—all
without negative consequences. He is convinced that he
knows what is best and when faced with a moral
dilemma, he will choose whatever serves himself. A
child's nature is to fight for immediate gratification.

Despite the dismal picture of mankind's utter depravity, each child is created by God to be good. Every child
bears His image and possesses a unique set of qualities
that prepare him or her for a special place in the Lord's
overall plan for the world.

As you reflect on the questions below, bear in mind
that the human author who wrote of man's depravity in
Psalms 51 and 58 also wrote Psalm 139.

**Read Psalm 139:13–16. According to Psalm 139:13,
who is responsible for the design and formation of a
child?**

What is the psalmist's opinion of God's creation in verse 14? Would you characterize his response as positive or negative?

Looking at verse 16, when did the Lord begin watching the child's development?

According to the same verse, what did the Lord do concerning the child's future?

If the Lord saw the child's destiny before he began to form, what does this suggest about the child's design?

GETTING TO THE ROOT

Notice the words the psalmist used throughout Psalm 139 to speak of God's direct involvement in His creation: "You formed," "You wove," "I was made," "I was wrought." Then in verse 16, he wrote, "And in Your book were all written the days that were ordained for me." Most English versions translate the Hebrew this way, but the literal meaning is more poetic. The Hebrew word used for "ordained" is *yatsar*, which means "to form or fashion"—like what an artisan does when he or she molds clay, weaves tapestry, or carves wood. And we find the very same root word used in Genesis 2:7 when God "formed man of dust from the ground."

Based on our study in Romans and the Psalms, we know that children are neither angels nor demons. They were created for good and possess great potential to fulfill the Lord's design. But they also have been thoroughly corrupted by sin and, consequently, can be capable of astonishing evil.

So where does that leave parents? We must adopt a balanced view of our children. This balance affects our attitude and guides our actions. Our efforts to encourage our child with grace and affirmation must not neglect the difficult task of correction.

STARTING YOUR JOURNEY

The Lord has given parents a huge stake in the process of curbing a child's evil bent while developing and encouraging the good He instilled within him or her. We cannot underestimate the importance of this role in a child's life. It requires lots of personal investment—our time, our emotional avail-ability, our deliberate awareness. While keeping the bal-anced view of Scripture in mind, consider these three points of action.

1. *Determine to know your child's uniqueness.*

 Reread Psalm 139:13–16, thinking about your child. How can you see God's design and pur-pose in his or her life? Be specific.

What activities can you do with your child that will help surface his or her interests and abilities?

2. *Discipline yourself to set limits on your child's will.*

Despite how hard children fight to have their own way, they long to have well-defined, unmovable bound-aries to help them make sense of the world around them. No child wants to be his or her own authority figure. Having no reliable, consistent person to give the world order and definition causes a child to grow increasingly insecure, fearful, defiant, and willful. Therefore, an indis-pensable task of the parent is to establish unambiguous standards of conduct, communicate them clearly, and then enforce them consistently. We'll discuss this further in the next lesson.

Leader Help

As a group exercise, think of a famous person, living or dead, known for his or her impact on the world. Draw a vertical line the length of a poster board to create two columns, la-beled "Positive" and "Neg-ative" respectively. Ask the group to list the positive and negative qualities of the individual based on their knowledge of history. Have them answer the question, "How did this person's unique set of qual-ities prepare him or her to impact the world?"

3. *Encourage your child and affirm his or her value.*

Encouragement praises what a child does, while affirmation praises who he or she is. Both are important and both require discernment. Encouraging a child without having observed him or her degenerates quickly to flattery, which only confuses a young person. Base your encouragement and affirmation on what you genuinely see.

List the positive qualities you see in your child—the traits that seem to be strong points in his or her character and abilities.

<u>Character Qualities</u>   <u>Abilities</u>

What specific things could you say or do to affirm your child's fundamental value to God? To you? Be creative! (You may want to consider Psalm 139:13–16 as you formulate your answer.)

When a child understands how God made him or her special, the child grows into an adult who knows how to establish personal boundaries. Boundaries provide a person the strength to stand his or her ground in the face of injustice, abuse, or attempted manipulation. People with personal boundaries are rarely taken advantage of because they have enough self-respect to give of themselves willingly.

When you determine to view your child through the balanced lens of Scripture—praising the good while curbing the evil bents—the gift you give your child is the gift of inner security and confidence.

As you determine to know your child's uniqueness, to discipline yourself to set limits on his or her will, and to affirm his or her value, take notes from the perfect Father. He knows you intimately, which puts Him in the best position to develop your maturity. He doesn't give you everything you want but never fails to meet your every need. And because He knows you, He knows the difference. His desire for you is that you grow into the kind of believer who enjoys the personality and the gifts He has given you, and He longs to see you fully alive. As the Lord develops your maturity, do the same for your child.

—*Parenting: From Surviving to Thriving*

Lesson Three

Establishing a Life of Self-Control

— Selected Proverbs —

THE HEART OF THE MATTER

Whether passed along by genetics or by influence—or whether it's something completely new to a family—an inclination toward one kind of sin or another is beyond a child's ability to curb. Therefore, parents must be watchful and then help their child to recognize sinful behavior, to know how it's triggered, and to learn how to exercise self-control. In the early years, this may require the use of corporal punishment (which is almost never effective or appropriate past the age of eleven.) However, any reprimand, especially if it involves spanking, must follow strict guidelines in order to have a positive effect.

To prepare for this lesson, read Proverbs 3:11–12; 23:13–14; and chapter 3 in *Parenting: From Surviving to Thriving.*

YOU ARE HERE

We discovered in our study in lesson two that all people are infected with the disease of sin. The problem of sin corrupts the nature of every person so that all people, even infants, possess a desire to please self, without regard for consequences. In this lesson, we will see

Leader Help

By the end of this lesson, group members should appreciate the necessity of corrective discipline, respect the guidelines for administering corrective discipline to achieve a constructive result, and commit themselves to correcting their children with consistency.

that certain kinds of sin (such as lying, substance abuse, or laziness) tend to be passed down from one generation to the next.

In Exodus 34:6–7, the Lord affirms His kindness and grace to forgive sin but says He will "by no means leave the guilty unpunished, visiting the iniquity of fathers on the children and on the grandchildren to the third and fourth generations." The Hebrew word translated "visit" means "to number, visit, be concerned with, look after, make a search for, punish."[1] While this may seem unfair at first glance, it is actually an expression of His grace.

The solution to curbing the evil bent and breaking destructive family legacies is consistent application of corrective discipline. Otherwise, an inclination toward certain kinds of sin in one generation tends to become a problem for the next. Perhaps you have seen this in your own experience.

What temptations, sins, or bad habits did your mother or father struggle with that also give you trouble?

If possible, have a conversation with your grandparents or parents. Did your grandparents struggle with the same sinful inclinations that afflicted your parents and you?

Do you see those tendencies in your child? Describe how this sinful inclination shows itself in his or her life.

Fast-forward to envision your child ten years from now. If you take no action to teach your child self-control by curbing this tendency, how might this sinful bent manifest itself in your child's future?

No parent with a right attitude toward discipline enjoys reprimanding a child; in fact, good parents loathe doing it. Nevertheless, corrective discipline is an act of love, as we see in the example of our heavenly Father, who disciplines those He loves (see Hebrews 12:7–11).

The word *discipline* is based on the same Latin root term as *disciple*. The purpose of discipline is instruction. And as any good mentor knows, discipline must be both formative and corrective. Formative discipline teaches, encourages, mentors, and inspires, while corrective discipline curbs bad behavior or replaces incorrect thinking with truth. This lesson examines corrective discipline while lesson four explores the role of formative discipline. (In this chapter, we use the terms *corporal punishment* and *spanking* to refer to a practice that falls under the umbrella of corrective discipline. This is but one of various corrective methods.)

Leader Help
Begin the meeting by having the group members share their immediate emotional response to the term *discipline*. Record the responses on a dry-erase board or a poster board and keep it visible during the lesson.

Examine your own family history and look for harmful tendencies that affected you. Determine, today, to keep them from becoming a problem for your children. This examination will give you the insight, the wisdom, and the compassion you need to rescue your children from the sins that plagued you, and your parents . . . and theirs.

—*Parenting: From Surviving to Thriving*

When done correctly, corporal punishment leaves the child humble, relieved, affirmed, and confident in his or her relationship with the parent. If you were spanked as a child, how did you typically feel during and after the experience?

As a result of your experience, do you (or do you plan to) use spanking as a parental tool? Why or why not?

In what circumstances should a parent avoid spanking a child?

DISCOVERING THE WAY

Advice on parental discipline can be found throughout the Scriptures; however, the Bible does not provide a how-to approach or offer specific methods of discipline. Instead, it describes the qualities that should characterize any form of discipline as well as the results it should achieve.

Read each passage listed below, and answer the corresponding question.

Proverbs 13:24—What is the proof of love according to this verse? In what respect is failing to discipline an act of hatred?

Proverbs 22:15—What is the purpose of corrective discipline?

Proverbs 23:13–14—What are the possible consequences for failing to administer an appropriate spanking?

Leader Help

The symbolism of the term "rod," which is used throughout the book of Proverbs, is largely lost on modern, Western culture, but it is vitally important to the meaning of Scripture. If a group member does not understand the full meaning of the term, his or her understanding of these proverbs will be skewed. Be sure to call the group members' attention to the "Getting to the Root" feature.

GETTING TO THE ROOT

The Hebrew word translated "rod" in most Bible versions refers to a wide range of wooden implements: a thick club, a short stick, a long pole. It was used to beat food such as dill and cumin

(Isaiah 28:7), as a weapon (2 Samuel 23:21), as a shepherd's staff (Psalm 23:4), and very often it referred to a scepter (Genesis 49:10). The rod was also used as an instrument of punishment of slaves (Exodus 21:20), of a fool (Proverbs 10:13), and of a son. Metaphorically, the rod symbolized protection, authority, and correction depending upon the context, and in some cases, it carried a sense of all three at once.

When used in connection with a parent, the rod often refers to discipline in the broadest sense: authority, leadership, correction (Proverbs 29:15). It usually refers to corrective action, including, but not limited to, corporal punishment (Proverbs 13:24, 19:18). And sometimes "the rod" is an expression for spanking (Proverbs 23:13–14), pointing to a neutral implement in the hands of an authority. In every such case, the rod is an instrument of love, never an outlet for parental anger. Its purpose is correction, never punishment for its own sake.

Dr. James Dobson explains the crucial role of corrective discipline this way:

> It is obvious that children are aware of the contest of wills between generations, and that is precisely why the parental response is so important. When a child behaves in ways that are disrespectful or harmful to himself or others, his hidden purpose is often to verify the stability of the boundaries. This testing has much the same function as a policeman who turns doorknobs at places of business after dark. Though he tries to open doors, he hopes they are locked and secure. Likewise, a child who assaults

> Unfortunately, spanking has become taboo in our society and, to some degree, I understand why. Far too many parents overuse and misapply it, even some well-meaning parents. Corporal punishment should be used only to correct defiance and curb direct disobedience. Furthermore, spanking is not merely hitting. Too often I'll see a mom or dad lean down and say in a stern voice, "I *told* you not to do that . . . (swat)!" The blow doesn't come as a lesson but as a punctuation mark. It's impulsive, rash, purposeless, often brutal, and only teaches the child to fear the parent.
> —*Parenting: From Surviving to Thriving*

the loving authority of his parents is greatly reassured when their leadership holds firm and confident. He finds his greatest security in a structured environment where the rights of other people (and his own) are protected by definite boundaries.[2]

 Read Ephesians 6:4 and Colossians 3:21. What are some errors a parent can make with regard to discipline that would cause a child legitimate anger, resentment, bitterness, or exasperation?

 What does Hebrews 12:11 say are the short-term versus long-term results of corrective discipline?

If a new parent were to ask for your advice, wondering, "What does the Bible say about spanking?" what would you say?

Using the rankings below, rate your willingness to apply corrective discipline (including spanking). Circle one.

    1—I refuse.

    2—I am very reluctant.

    3—I am indifferent.

    4—I don't like it, but I acknowledge it is important.

    5—I believe corrective discipline is crucial if my child is going to learn self-control.

Explain:

As you reflect on the generational sins or tendencies in your family and consider your observations about your child's personality, what form of corrective discipline is best suited to help your child learn healthy self-control?

STARTING YOUR JOURNEY

Scripture commands corrective discipline as a parental duty and as an act of love. Of course, spanking is only one form of reprimand. Others include grounding, issuing a time-out, removing privileges or pleasures for a time, adding extra chores—any penalty we compound to whatever negative consequences already come as a result of a child's poor choices. Ephesians 6:4 and Colossians 3:21 urge parents to discipline children in such a way as to avoid exasperating them or provoking them to anger. Our purpose is to instruct our children without stripping their confidence or planting seeds of anger. To do that, we must apply any form of corrective discipline responsibly and wisely.

Applying the "Rod" Responsibly

Too often, corrective discipline—especially corporal punishment—fails to accomplish its purpose, even causing the very behaviors we hope to avoid. Sometimes the child is particularly strong-willed, but usually a failure on the part of the parent to observe some basic guidelines is to blame. When applying corrective discipline of any kind, consider the following essential guidelines.

1. *Be faithful and consistent.*

Children long to have their parents take the time to set boundaries, instruct them, and even reprimand them when the boundaries are crossed. While the experience is unpleasant in the short term, children instinctively feel that their worth has been affirmed. Furthermore, when the rules and the consequences remain consistent—what deserved reproof yesterday earns the same reproof today—the world becomes knowable. Living in a world with slippery standards leaves the child feeling defeated, exasperated, excitable, and even angry.

Leader Help

This section does not include questions as in other lessons. As the leader, during group time, walk through the guidelines and procedure without reading them in full, and invite group members to pose questions or offer their perspectives along the way. As an extra help in answering questions, consider inviting to your meeting an older couple who has successfully reared children who now have families of their own.

2. Stay clear of abuse.

A definite line divides discipline from abuse. Here are some distinctions to keep in mind:

Abuse is cruel.	Discipline is corrective.
Abuse is unfair.	Discipline is fair.
Abuse is extreme (too long, too harsh).	Discipline is measured (reasonable).
Abuse leaves marks.	Discipline is harmless.
Abuse damages self-worth.	Discipline affirms self-worth.

3. Never punish childish irresponsibility.

An important distinction exists between capriciousness and disobedience. Discerning parents learn to handle this difference with care. Dr. James Dobson explains:

When [a child] forgets to feed the dog or make his bed or take out the trash—when he leaves your tennis racket outside in the rain or loses his bicycle—remember that these behaviors are typical of childhood. . . . Be gentle as you teach him to do better. If he fails to respond to your patient instruction, it then becomes appropriate to administer some well-defined consequences (he may have to work to pay for the item he abused or be deprived of its use, etc.). However, childish irresponsibility is very different from willful defiance, and should be handled more patiently.[3]

4. *Break the will, not the spirit.*

The purpose of corrective discipline is to reestablish authority by temporarily breaking the child's will—teaching the child to recognize when he or she is wrong and to surrender to appropriate authority. On the other hand, we never want to break a child's spirit. A child whose spirit has been broken lives without the hope of ever succeeding, of ever knowing how to "be good" and to please Mom and Dad. A broken spirit is the result of continually exasperating a child.

Applying the "Rod" with Wisdom

Having an established method for applying corrective discipline will help keep it reasonable and productive. Diligently adhering to a set of steps not only provides consistent reinforcement for the child, it serves as a reality check for the parent. Let's face it, parents can, in their sinfulness, turn correction into a convenient way to dominate rather than instruct, or allow emotions to unduly affect the opportunity to teach. Consider following these steps each time you must apply corrective discipline.

1. *Explain the offense.*

When emotions have settled, take the child aside, get down at eye level with him or her, and in a low, reasonable, sympathetic tone, explain the offense and the need for corrective discipline. This must be done in private—embarrassing the child will squelch your message. Be sure to point out that the boundary and the consequence of crossing it was clearly discussed beforehand.

2. *Set the time and parameters.*

If at all possible, the discipline should be administered immediately. But if circumstances prevent immediate discipline, tell the child what will happen and when.

Keep your expectations for the child appropriate for his or her age, and tailor your punishment accordingly. As one wise grandmother advised her daughter on child-rearing, "Try not to see *everything.*" Keep your cool. Anger not only frightens children, it stops up their ears. They can't hear past your emotions, so if you want them to hear, speak and act calmly.

—*Parenting: From Surviving to Thriving*

3. *Apply the penalty.*

Follow through on what you have stated, promptly and exactly. Your actions must reflect your words so that, in time, your child knows that what you say is no less certain than reality.

4. *Affirm the child.*

After corrective discipline, a child will naturally wonder if you still like him or her. Once the consequences have been administered and the child has had time to settle down, affirm him or her without going back to the offense. An apology from the child at this point is inappropriate as he or she has just paid a penalty for wrongdoing. Instead, affirm your child with your love and your belief in his or her ability to do well in the future.

5. *Close the matter.*

After affirming your child, prompt whatever activity comes next. Move on with life. In this way, you are demonstrating by your actions that the matter is settled, that there's no need to discuss it again (unless the child brings it up), and that you are focused on moving forward. Invite him or her to help you with dinner, offer to read a story later, or engage him or her in an age-appropriate activity that involves you both. You will likely find that your relationship will be very tender and sweet during this time.

Leader Help

Call the group's attention to their responses to the word *discipline,* which you recorded at the beginning of the lesson. En-courage them to describe how their impressions have changed, if at all.

Wherever you are in the childrearing process, remember, it's never too late to start doing what is right. You may be hindered by thoughts that suddenly implementing a consistent method of corrective discipline will make you look foolish to your child. His or her reaction will likely include confusion and doubt at first, but your child will quickly adapt. Consistency breeds confidence, which grows into trust. This occurs much faster for children than for adults, so the younger they are, the more quickly the trust will grow.

Therefore:

Start early. Start right away. Don't delay. Every moment you have with your child is an opportunity to invest in his or her growth and success.

Stay balanced. Preface the rod with plenty of reproof (verbal instruction). Corrective discipline cannot substitute for a relationship; in fact, corrective discipline without a relationship only breeds anger. Positive instruction, encouragement, and affirmation should outweigh correction ten to one.

Be consistent. Clearly establish boundaries and expectations, keeping them consistent with all siblings (adjusting for age, of course), and apply consequences faithfully.

Remain reasonable. Keep your expectations within reason for the child's age and abilities. And remain calm. Never allow emotions to affect the consistency of the discipline.

Our ultimate desire is to teach our children self-control. As humans, we all want to have what we want, when we want it, with no cost to pay. However, maturity is defined as the ability to control our impulses and to foresee the consequences of our actions. With self-control comes the capacity to enjoy helpful instruction, greater freedom, and ever-increasing blessing.

Lesson Four

Cultivating a Life of Self-Worth

— Proverbs 4:20–27 —

THE HEART OF THE MATTER

At the heart of a healthy sense of self-worth is a twelve-word maxim that guides the daily existence of emotionally healthy people, though few put words to it. The maxim is "Know who you are; accept who you are; be who you are." This is the essence of authentic living, which goes hand in hand with a robust self-esteem.

Children are born with an identity—a unique combination of temperament, interests, abilities, and style—that forms the basis of their relationship with God and others. But they aren't born knowing who they are. The Lord gave them parents to help them discover their identity as people in Christ and as unique individuals destined for a place in His kingdom.

Our job as parents is to guide our children toward self-knowledge and self-acceptance so that they can have the strength to live authentically. Authentic living is the best way to build a healthy self-image.

To prepare for this lesson, read Proverbs 4:20–27 and chapter 4 in *Parenting: From Surviving to Thriving*.

Leader Help

By the end of this lesson, group members should accept the maxim "Know who you are; accept who you are; be who you are" as a guiding principle in child-rearing, understand the concept of authenticity, and commit themselves to being authentic with their children.

YOU ARE HERE

In his commentary on Galatians, William Barclay includes this story of Benjamin West, a brilliant painter who lived around the time of the American Revolution. A remarkable incident involving the artist's mother encouraged him to explore his talent.

One day his mother went out leaving him in charge of his little sister Sally. In his mother's absence he discovered some bottles of coloured ink and began to paint Sally's portrait. In the doing so he made a very considerable mess of things with ink blots all over. His mother came back. She saw the mess, but she said nothing. She picked up the piece of paper and saw the drawing. "Why," she said, "it's Sally!" and she stooped and kissed him. Ever after Benjamin West used to say: "My mother's kiss made me a painter."[1]

Building One Another

As parents, we desire that our children listen closely to our counsel, benefit from our wisdom that came by experience, make wise choices, and avoid the mistakes we made. Therefore, it's easy to find ourselves interacting with our children only when we see a problem. We step in to point out the error, hoping that they will hear our correction and follow a better course. Instead, defenses go up, excuses are made, and rationalizations follow. Then come heated words, hurt feelings, and a hasty retreat in wounded silence. If our children hear from us only when they have blown it, they can begin to resent our presence. Who wouldn't?

Romans 14:19 says, "So then we pursue the things which make for peace and the building up of one another." The question we, as parents, must continually ask ourselves is, "Am I building up my child with my words, or am I tearing him or her down?"

 Thinking back over the last week or two, what usually prompted a conversation with your child?

Generally speaking, which did the conversations involve—something positive or negative about him or her?

❑   Positive   ❑   Negative

About how long do your conversations with your child typically last?

How would you describe your feelings after the conversations with your child?

Leader Help

Provide each group member with a set of note cards. On one side of each card, write the name of a group member; on the other write, "Something I admire about you." Each group member should have one card for each of the other members. Have them complete the cards anonymously and place them in a container. At various times throughout your meeting, pull a card from the container and read it to the group. At the end of the meeting, read any remaining cards and be sure each person receives his or her cards. The power of affirmation will be self-evident.

How do you imagine your child feels about himself or herself, about you, and about your relationship after the conversations?

If your child were to base his or her self-image entirely upon your words and demeanor toward him or her, describe the person he or she would see.

⌐

As parents, we have the opportunity to help our offspring know their value, their worth, which gives them the confidence to become whatever God made them to be. If they don't learn it at home, they can easily become lost, confused victims of midlife crisis. How rare are parents who deliberately give their child the gift of personal identity.

—*Parenting: From Surviving to Thriving*

 ## DISCOVERING THE WAY

Criticism is occasionally a necessary part of childrearing. A glance at the past gives a child some much-needed correction. However, guiding a child toward responsible, healthy adulthood using only criticism is like driving a car forward while using only the rearview mirror! Cultivating a child's self-worth is crucial if we expect them to keep heading in the right direction.

The way forward need not include empty affirmation or meaningless flattery, as many contemporary "experts" seem to advocate. Proverbs 4:20–27 records the ancient words of a father to his son, and in these verses we find a more effective way to cultivate a child's self-worth. This father chose to build his son through the discipline of authenticity. He wanted to teach his child how to develop integrity and how to be himself—a monumental task for everyone, not just young people.

How to Cultivate a Child's Self-Worth

1. *Teach authenticity.*

In Proverbs 4:20–22, the father pleads with his child to heed his counsel.

 Read Proverbs 4:20–22. How important would you say the father considers his advice to his child? What words or phrases support your answer?

If the child hears the father's words yet sees that he fails to live them out, how is the child likely to behave?

How is the child to learn about life and how to make wise choices?

To be nobody-but-yourself—in a world which is doing its best, night and day, to make you everybody else—means to fight the hardest battle which any human being can fight; and never stop fighting.

—*e. e. cummings*[2]

For our words to have substance, they must have life—authentic, real, unvarnished, flawed experience. When we blow it, say, "I blew it." When we're wrong, say, "I was wrong." When we offend our children, we need to own the harm we caused and deliberately seek their forgiveness. When we are struggling with life, we need not hide all of it. They need to see us wrestle with problems, put our concerns before God in prayer, learn the lessons He has to teach, and overcome them in God's power—all before their eyes. Let them see your spiritual life as it is, warts and all. Children need to know that parents don't have all of life wired up tight. Phony parents rear phony kids.

—*Parenting: From Surviving to Thriving*

---

2. *Be authentic.*

In Proverbs 4:23–25, the father encourages his child to live authentically, that is, from the heart and according to truth. Note the progression: heart (4:23), speech (4:24), direction (4:25). *Merriam-Webster's Dictionary* defines *authenticity* as "worthy of acceptance or belief as conforming to or based on fact; . . . not false or imitation; true to one's own personality, spirit, or character."[3] Living authentically means one's actions faithfully reflect what's in the heart.

The Hebrew for the first phrase of Proverbs 4:23 reads, literally, "More than all guarding, preserve your heart." One Hebrew way to emphasize a point is to double and redouble the words. "First, foremost, and above all," he says, "guard your heart!"

Most parents tell their children to "behave themselves," that is, to make sure their actions are morally upright. What does this father tell his child in verse 23?

When a person lives life authentically, what is the relationship between his or her heart and actions?

What effect would the habit of living authentically have on the self-esteem and confidence of a child?

When a child is taught to put on a mask or to become what others expect rather than to be himself or herself, how does it affect the child's self-image?

If a child cannot *be* herself, how likely is she to *know* and *accept* herself?

3. *Reward obedience.*

Proverbs 4:25–27 teaches the child to make progress by fixing his eyes on where he should go (4:25), making his feet follow his sight (4:26), and experiencing the positive outcome (4:27). Hand in hand with his teaching on the heart, Solomon calls his son to righteous behavior. He issues a warning against evil ways and also emphasizes the rewards of a godly lifestyle: "all your ways will be established" (4:26). The discipline process—both correction and affirmation—is the parent's way of allowing his or her child to learn by experience.

GETTING TO THE ROOT

Proverbs 4:26 says, "Watch the path of your feet and all your ways will be established." The Hebrew word translated "be established" means "set up, accomplish, do, make firm, make ready, prepare, provide, provide for, furnish."[4] The form of the verb lends itself to what scholars call "the divine passive," which is to suggest that the action will be accomplished by the Lord, even though He is not named specifically. The child is told, by the use of wordplay, that by keeping his eye on the path, his ways (*derek*) will be established. We learned earlier that *derek* can mean a literal path or a characteristic manner.

In other words, by walking the path successfully, the child's character will be developed and made firm by the Lord.

 Consider an example of a time when you chose to obey God or to do the right thing and were rewarded. What effect did it have on your self-esteem and confidence?

When a child is encouraged to make a plan, take a step, and experience success, how does it affect his or her self-esteem and confidence?

When self-esteem is absent, various signs of insecurity present themselves. Do you recognize any of these behavior patterns in your child?

____ Bullying or attempting to dominate

____ Submitting to unhealthy extremes or permitting mistreatment

____Wearing masks

____Conforming to peer pressure

____Being a clown or acting out to garner attention

When a child's ways are "established" by the Lord (see "Getting to the Root"), how will it affect his or her courage in the face of temptation or peer pressure?

The context of Proverbs 4:20–27 is moral integrity, yet the principles have broader application. Reread the passage as though the father were giving his child advice about choosing and pursuing a vocation. Paraphrase the passage to reflect the counsel you would give your child.

We learned in lesson one that the best-kept secret of wise parenting is this: "The job of a parent is to help his or her children come to know themselves, grow to like themselves, and find satisfaction in being themselves."

Put another way, the goal we have for our children is authentic living based on a relationship with the Lord and a life built on integrity. To give our children this gift, we must be authentic ourselves, teach them authenticity, and then reward them for the wise choices they make.

STARTING YOUR JOURNEY

The value of a healthy self-worth to a child cannot be measured. Children who lack a good understanding of their identity, or who are too insecure to be who they are, can grow into adults who possess pathological defense mechanisms, flimsy personal boundaries, or a compulsion to wear masks in order to be acceptable to all. All of these are the enemies of authenticity.

On the other hand, people with healthy self-esteem know who they are, feel no need to defend or justify themselves, feel no pressure to perform for the sake of others, and have the ability to feel and express the full range of human emotions. What they are on the outside reflects who they are on the inside. Teaching a child how to be authentic begins early.

1. *Teach authenticity.*

Prior to the age of eleven or twelve, children cannot process abstract concepts; so when it comes to Christian spirituality, words mean very little. They believe what they see demonstrated and they comprehend what they accomplish. In order to teach authenticity, we must make the effort to connect words with action.

> Someone who accepts and likes himself has the ability to love others unselfishly. Someone who believes she is worthy of compassion has compassion to give. Furthermore, accepting and liking who we are honors the God who created us. We validate the fact that He makes no mistakes and that we have worth just as we are.
>
> —*Parenting: From Surviving to Thriving*

For each of the Christian values below, think of an activity that you and your child can do together that will allow him or her to see it in action. Don't be afraid to ask for suggestions and to share your ideas with others.

Love

Peace

Generosity

Kindness

Faithfulness

Gentleness

Mercy

Honesty

Every child has a unique learning style—some learn by hearing, some are visual learners, some are more "hands-on." Observe what captivates your child's attention. How can you incorporate his or her learning style as you teach your child?

 What activity or endeavor that you find fulfilling can you share with your child?

How might seeing your pleasure and fulfillment influence your child's growth?

2. Be authentic.

We must not teach what we do not practice, especially when the subject is authenticity. Children typically ignore what we say and mimic what we do. Therefore, we must model the behavior we hope to see in them. If we want them to listen, we must learn to listen. If we want them to accept correction gracefully, we must accept it gracefully. This may require an openness with your child to which neither of you are accustomed.

Below are a few suggestions for how you can model authenticity in your relationship. Explain how each suggestion will enhance your child's self-esteem as well as his or her respect for you.

- Allow your child to express his or her honest opinions without reprisal, even if they are about you. Resist the temptation to counterargue. Instead, express admiration for his or her effort to think about things. Ask questions to keep him or her talking. Find an insight to praise.

- Respond to criticism from your child by listening carefully, even when it's offered with a poor attitude. Then respond with the words, "Thank you for being honest with me." Choose to address the poor attitude at a later date.

- When you must correct your child's behavior, begin with something positive and avoid the word *but*. (This will require forethought and a lot of creativity. Try using the word *and*.

- If you get your facts wrong about something or your opinion proves to be faulty, be quick to admit it. Children instinctively know that Mom or Dad can't know everything.

- If you offend, be quick to apologize using the words, "I was wrong. Will you forgive me?"

- Avoid squelching your child's emotion. Allow him or her to fully express anger, fear, sorrow, joy, etc. Emotions don't get out of control when they are expressed, only when squelched, ignored, or

Leader Help

Ask the group members which of the suggestions makes them uncomfortable and why. Ask them to share which suggestions they have applied with success and to reflect on the experience.

ridiculed. Emotions quickly subside when heard with empathy. Try to understand what truth the emotions point to.

3. *Reward obedience.*

Very often, success is its own reward. When a child experiences the exhilaration of doing something well, he or she will be looking for another opportunity to repeat it. Success builds confidence, enhances self-esteem, reinforces good behavior, and when *you* are involved, successfully accomplishing something worthy creates an opportunity to bond.

List the positive qualities you see in your child.

During the coming week, find opportunities to compliment your child using something you listed above. Keep it simple and brief. "I really admire how hard you try at school. I'm very proud of you."

Sometimes, big achievements call for something special. Years ago, the Swindoll family adopted an early American tradition called the red plate:

When you want to honor someone for a special day, a significant achievement, or simply to encourage him or her, set the table as you normally would, only place a red plate before the person of honor. Not long ago, we took one of our grown children to dinner at a favorite restaurant because we wanted to give her something special that we wanted her to enjoy. She suspected nothing until the waiter brought her food on the Red Plate. Her reaction was not unusual. Her eyes immediately filled with tears. The full impact of this family tradition told her what we wanted her to hear: "You are very special."[5]

Become your child's loudest cheerleader. Applaud his independence, praise her initiative, and lavish your admiration upon your child when he or she chooses to stand alone against peer pressure. Find ways to catch your child doing something right, and be sure others see it too. In time, your child will know himself, like himself, and will have the courage to be himself. He or she will always remember you as the one who helped him or her cultivate a life of self-worth.

Lesson Five

Secret Struggles . . . Family Troubles

— 2 Samuel 13 —

THE HEART OF THE MATTER

Because all families are composed of imperfect people, perfect families do not exist.

Some families experience more difficulties than others; however, we cannot tell by appearances which are dysfunctional and which are reasonably healthy. The worst kind of evil can be found in the most respectable home.

Very often, extreme dysfunction begins with something small, a seemingly insignificant transgression or tendency that remains unaddressed. On the surface, everything appears to be completely unaffected by the sin. But unresolved evil has consequences that fester and cause more complications. If the sin is left unresolved long enough, the eventual fallout can be sudden and devastating.

Passivity in the face of sin can destroy a family, leaving its members to become progressively dysfunctional. Parents must be courageous, uncover and acknowledge unpleasant truths, and appropriately address evil wherever they find it, beginning with themselves.

To prepare for this lesson, read 2 Samuel 13 and chapter 5 in *Parenting: From Surviving to Thriving*.

Leader Help

By the end of this lesson, group members should accept that evil never re-solves itself and that passivity on the part of the parent will allow evil to fester. They should assume an active role in identifying and addressing any moral wrongs within their family promptly and decisively.

YOU ARE HERE

Merriam-Webster's Collegiate Dictionary defines *authentic* as "worthy of acceptance or belief as conforming to or based on fact, not false or imitation: real, actual."[1] Let's face it, none of us wants to look bad, especially in front of our neighbors and friends. It's normal to try to maintain a certain dignity for the outside world when, in fact, our household may not be completely in order. However, the real question is, *how authentic is your family with itself?*

As a parent, the responsibility is yours to discern the truth and to uncover and address wrong. To remain passive toward sin is to teach your children that wrongdoing is acceptable, which quite often leads to anger, depression, and rebellion among children. How willing are you to overcome this temptation? How willing are you to discover and accept the unvarnished truth that your family may not be as healthy as you would like to believe? One author wrote, "We lie loudest when we lie to ourselves"[2] and, "To most of us nothing is so invisible as an unpleasant truth."[3]

 How would you gauge the emotional climate of your household? Place an X along the line to indicate your assessment.

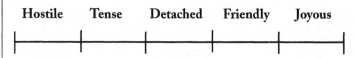

Hostile	Tense	Detached	Friendly	Joyous

From your perspective, which two people in your family enjoy the best relationship with each other?

Leader Help

After four meetings, the group should be reasonably comfortable discussing sensitive issues. Use the first question as an icebreaker. As individuals answer and appear concerned about a less-than-friendly atmosphere, invite them to elaborate. Be careful to limit the discussion time.

Describe what you see as the best qualities of their relationship.

From your perspective, which two people in your family have a relationship with each other that needs some improvement?

From what you know, what causes them the most difficulty in relating to each other?

To your knowledge, does any member of the family feel that a sin against him or her has not been resolved to his or her satisfaction?

❑   Yes   ❑   No

If you answered yes, describe the situation and why it has not been resolved.

All families—famous or infamous, affluent or needy, black, Asian, white, Middle Eastern, interracial, churched, nonreligious, or pagan—they all struggle with selfishness and interpersonal strife. That's because 100 percent of all families are filled with people whose natures have been entirely corrupted by sin from the moment of conception.

—*Parenting: From Surviving to Thriving*

What possible complications could arise if the difficulty is not resolved?

David's character, like mine and yours, had some very significant blots. The Holy Spirit inspired the human author to include these unflattering details for our benefit, so that we can observe where David failed in his role as father and avoid the heartbreak that eroded his family relationships and fractured his nation. We best honor the hero by rising above his failings.

—*Parenting: From Surviving to Thriving*

DISCOVERING THE WAY

Second Samuel 13 records a terrible incident involving the royal family as well as David's passive response as both father and king. The turmoil in David's household illustrates two important principles. First, *the worst kind of evil can be found in the most respected homes.* Some families, even those we would never suspect—powerful world leaders, pastors, respected corporate leaders—harbor the most shameful family secrets. Second, and most important to our lesson, *unresolved evil has consequences that fester and cause more complications.* Sins that are not addressed and brought to an appropriate resolution can silently destroy family ties and encourage more sin.

 According to 2 Samuel 3:2–3, who was Absalom's mother?

Who was Amnon's mother?

According to 2 Samuel 13:1, how were Tamar and Amnon related?

David's firstborn son, Amnon, was born to David and Ahinoam during the earliest years of David's reign, before his move to Jerusalem, before his long absences from home, before the hectic demands of leading the nation and before he indulged his lust with a harem of more than a dozen women. By the time of 2 Samuel 13, brothers Absalom and Amnon were full-grown men.

How might Amnon's upbringing and childhood environment have influenced his attitude toward women?

Based on your reading of 2 Samuel 13:10–14, describe the contrast you see between Amnon's character and Tamar's.

Leader Help

Parenting: From Surviving to Thriving contains a chart in chapter 5 illustrating the size and complexity of David's household. As a group, use a blank poster board and paper doll cutouts to replicate David's family tree using the Scripture references listed at the top of the chart. As an alternative, you may wish to replicate it on a white board. Have the group members describe how they would feel if a family like this moved into their neighborhood.

According to 2 Samuel 13:21–23, what was David's response to this family strife? What did he do to give Tamar justice?

How long did Absalom wait for David to give Tamar justice? How did this affect his attitude toward Amnon? How do you think he felt about his father?

 According to 2 Samuel 13:28–29, how did Tamar receive justice for the crime against her?

According to 2 Samuel 13:31–39, how did David respond to the murder of Amnon? What did he do about it?

How did David feel about Absalom's self-imposed exile? What did he do about it?

 Based on your study of 2 Samuel 13, how would you describe David as a parent?

Read 1 Kings 1:6 regarding David and his son Adonijah. Describe David's attitude toward sin in his household.

Summarize in your own words the effect that David's attitude and response toward wrongdoing had on his family. How did it affect their actions? Their character?

DOORWAY TO HISTORY

In my forty-plus years in pastoral ministry, I have seen secret struggles and family troubles that would boggle the mind. I wish that I could say that the Bible's portrayal of David's difficulties were extreme for the sake of making an impression, but it is not. The destructive power of sin left to run unchecked can do the same, and worse, in any family.

—Parenting: From Surviving to Thriving

The kingdom of Geshur lay within the boundaries of Israel, occupying land allotted to the half tribe of Manasseh during the Israelites' initial conquest of Canaan. God had commanded Israel to expel *all* of the inhabitants of Canaan because they were extremely immoral and would prove to be a dangerous influence on the Hebrew people (Deuteronomy 9:4). Furthermore, the Lord had commanded Israel not to make covenants with the Canaanites (Deuteronomy 7:2; Judges 2:2) or to intermarry with them (Deuteronomy 7:3; Joshua 23:12–13), but to drive them out completely (Deuteronomy 7:2, 24). The Israelites never finished the difficult task of expelling the inhabitants (Joshua 13:13; Judges 1:27), so Geshur remained a sovereign realm within Israel through the period of the judges and into David's reign.

David could have obeyed the Lord's command and completed the conquest by driving out the Geshurites soon after he received the crown. Instead, he compounded Israel's disobedience. Despite God's strict orders to avoid treaties and intermarriage, David married King Talmai's daughter Maacah, probably sealing a nonaggression treaty between the two nations.

As we noted at the beginning, *unresolved evil has consequences that fester and cause more complications.* When they took the Promised Land, Israel tolerated the infectious presence of the pagan Geshurites. Hundreds of years later, David married the daughter of the pagan king of Geshur, who gave safe haven to Absalom, a product of this forbidden union. We can only guess at how much Absalom's three years in Geshur influenced his decision to undermine David and lead a rebellion to drive him out.

The Bible never glorifies its heroes. Throughout Scripture we can see that the very finest men and women were capable of sin, just as we are. In the case of David, the "man after [God's] own heart" (1 Samuel 13:14) and Israel's greatest king until the birth of Christ, we discover his parenting skills to be sadly lacking. His failure to engage his children and his passivity in dealing with unpleasant truths helped to destroy the lives of several children and ripped his nation in two.

Our purpose is not to criticize David so we can feel superior. In fact, despite his obvious flaws, we would do well to be more like him. We must examine the unpleasant truths in David's life, as well as in our own, so that we do not repeat his mistakes. We honor the memory of this great man by allowing his life to edify ours.

STARTING YOUR JOURNEY

If we are honest with ourselves, most of us can identify with David's passivity. David's story lets us see the potentially deadly result of passive parenting, even in the home of an acknowledged man of God. His experience also points to no fewer than three warnings for any parent who might be tempted to neglect his or her role as protector and guide.

1. *Disconnected and damaged relationships at home result in dysfunctional family members.*

Tim Kimmel explained this warning well in his book *Why Christian Kids Rebel.*

It's a strange thing about our parental sins. When our kids move away and we haven't resolved our sins of commission or omission with them, these childhood disappointments grow larger and larger until they dominate our kids' focus and dictate many of

Leader Help

Be careful with this section—you may encounter parental guilt or defensiveness. To accomplish the teaching objectives, focus only on those individuals who appear to be relaxed discussing their parental errors.

their actions. In fact, our unwillingness to try to make peace with our kids before they leave home can set them up for a lifetime of bad decisions.[4]

As far as you know, have you done anything either to hurt or to offend your child? If you resolved the matter, describe how you went about resolving it. Is the matter still unresolved? Why?

As far as you know, have you remained passive to the harm done to your child by a sibling or other family member? How have you or how will you begin to resolve the matter?

 Which statement best describes your attitude when you have hurt or offended your child?

❑ My child is too young or immature to understand the offense, so I see no need to address it. I will simply avoid repeating the mistake.

❑ If I accept complete blame for my actions, my child will think less of me and will lose respect for me.

David's fatal flaw as a parent was his passivity. He conquered nations and built the kingdom, but he left his family to solve its own problems and mature itself. But children can't rear themselves. They need more than food, water, and shelter; they need us.

—*Parenting: From Surviving to Thriving*

❑ I feel so terrible about what I've done that I can't face my child. He or she will reject me.

❑ I am truly remorseful for what I did. My child deserves to hear me apologize so he or she can recover and heal faster. Our relationship is worth my humiliation.

❑ If I admit to being completely wrong, my child will exploit the situation, and I won't be in charge.

❑ I might as well accept responsibility for my actions because my child can see that I'm at fault. Maybe he or she will respect me for addressing it rather than ignoring it or placing some or all blame on him or her.

If you remain passive and do not resolve a sin against your child, how might this affect his or her other relationships? Use your imagination and be as detailed as possible.

How might unresolved sin between you and your child affect the child's relationship with God?

In order to cultivate genuine closeness within the family, parents must be willing to face difficult truths and follow through with decisive action. This may require

If we're brutally honest with ourselves, we have to admit that the problems our children present to us can feel like tasks added to an already over-burdened list. So we prioritize our days, listing unpleasant items near the bottom, resolving to give them due attention if they begin to approach a crisis level. Meanwhile, the child hears the message we have sent: *You are less important than the project I must complete by next Wednesday.*
     —*Parenting: From Surviving to Thriving*

vulnerability with our children and admitting wrong
(without requiring them to be at fault . . . even a little,
without justifying our actions, and without making
excuses).

*2. Passive, permissive parents produce angry, frustrated
children.*

**Does your child seem angry or frustrated much of the
time, or does he or she struggle with temperamental out-
bursts? Describe the behaviors you see.**

**What keeps you from getting involved? There may
be more than one answer to this question.**

If your children are often angry and frustrated, look
within yourself. Have you remained passive or uninvolved
despite the troubles you have seen them struggling to
overcome? A good place to start might be a calm conversation with your child. The following approach may be
helpful:

- Affirm your love for your child and describe how
  important he or she is to you.
- Apologize and accept responsibility if you have
  been distracted or disconnected from your child.

- Assure your child that he or she is not in trouble and state how much you care.
- With empathy and a sympathetic tone, describe the behavior you have seen lately and why it does not reflect the child you know him or her to be.
- Ask your child to describe what might be troubling him or her.
- Listen, listen, listen.

The purpose of the conversation is to help your child to talk freely, which will be difficult and awkward at first, especially if the issue is embarrassing or traumatic. Say as little as possible, using only enough words to encourage your child to be vulnerable. Allow your patient silence and your affection to give your child the feeling of safety. If and when he or she begins to talk, do anything you can to prevent interruption until everything has been said. Limit your responses to statements of affirmation and gratitude. For example, "That must have been very painful for you. Thank you for being honest with me."

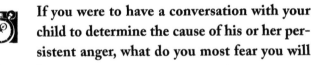 **If you were to have a conversation with your child to determine the cause of his or her persistent anger, what do you most fear you will discover?**

3. *Unresolved and unreconciled conflicts create wounds that never heal themselves.*

As much as we would like the problems to just go away, conflicts have a way of festering.

As you have studied this lesson, have you discovered that a hurt or offense between members of your household has not been resolved? Describe the offense.

How does the lack of resolution affect their relationship and the general mood of the home? You may have to ask questions and probe the situation before answering.

What can you do, and how might your involvement help rebuild the relationship?

As you begin to face difficult truths and resolve interpersonal offenses in your household, beware of these common rationalizations. Don't allow yourself or your children to fall victim to them.

- "He's the one who owes me an apology! The first move is his."
- "When she wants to get serious about this relationship, I'm here. I'll wait her out."
- "This is not a big deal; it'll resolve itself if I give it time."

- "Hey, nobody's perfect. Compared to _____, I'm doing pretty well."
- "That's ancient history; nobody even remembers it. Why dig up old trouble?"
- "Everybody in our family is a Christian. Each person can take his wounds directly to the Lord."

Each of these rationalizations can cloud the truth, allowing unresolved evil to fester and produce more complications.

~~~

If David could have seen the horrific results of allowing evil to go unaddressed in his family, he very likely would have made different choices. Now that you have seen the tragedy that can occur in even the best of families, you have a responsibility. Refuse to remain passive. Choose to act.

Lesson Six

From Resentment to Rebellion

— Selections from 2 Samuel 14–18 —

THE HEART OF THE MATTER

King David's passivity as a father left his son Absalom to stew in his resentment for many years. Despite repeated attempts by Absalom and his intermediaries to pursue reconciliation, David refused to see his son. Guilt and shame kept him from admitting the truth of his failures and bridging the ever-widening gap between him and his son. Eventually, Absalom's resentment turned into rebellion, culminating in a life-and-death struggle between father and son that plunged the nation into civil war. While Absalom's response to David's injustice and passivity was his own responsibility, we must accept that David's role was definitive.

When a child rebels, the parent bears a significant share of the responsibility. The outcome could have been much different if David had been willing to face difficult truths, accept responsibility for his failings as a parent, and reestablish a relationship with his son.

To prepare for this lesson, please read 2 Samuel 14:21–15:37; 16:15–23; 18:1–33; and chapter 6 in *Parenting: From Surviving to Thriving.*

Leader Help

By the end of this lesson, group members should recognize that parents bear a significant share of the responsibility for childhood rebellion and that fractured relationships begin to heal when we are willing to hear and admit the truth. They should decide to end attempts to control and manipulate their children and should commit to addressing any resentment their children may bear.

YOU ARE HERE

Two people can live in close proximity to each other yet keep a cool distance emotionally. And when this occurs between a parent and his or her child, the consequences can be devastating.

Often, an offense on the part of the parent causes the child to feel resentment, primarily because the child has very little ability to address wrongs with an adult. They lack the skills and the wisdom, and they are usually too afraid to try. Left unresolved, resentment almost always grows into rebellion. Therefore, the parent must take the lead.

This can be very difficult for a number of reasons. First, children have difficulty explaining their hurts well enough for adults to understand, so they often carry their wounds in silence. A parent might take the silence to mean that everything is well when, in fact, the wound he or she caused may be festering. Second, taking ownership for an offense against a child requires considerable vulnerability, which *Merriam-Webster's Dictionary* defines as the quality of being "open to attack or damage: assailable."[1]

Nevertheless, when a breach occurs, we parents must close the gap between us and our children. If we don't, we become primarily responsible for the rebellion that our passivity may spark.

 Suppose you were to experience a fracture in your relationship with your child. Describe what you believe would be the greatest difficulty in repairing it.

Thinking about your relationships in general, how open to criticism are you? How do you typically react when approached with a grievance?

Which one of the following responses best describes you, in general?

❑ I usually feel responsible when there's a conflict, so I admit I'm wrong when I'm not completely sure.

❑ I have been wrong so many times, I'm used to it. I'm very quick to admit when I'm at fault.

❑ Admitting that I have done something wrong is uncomfortable, but I generally own up to what I have done because it's better in the long run.

❑ I would rather eat sawdust than have to admit I'm wrong, even when I know I'm at fault.

❑ When I know I am wrong, I won't admit it right away but will often come back later and admit my error.

❑ I don't have a problem admitting when I'm wrong about my facts, but I have difficulty admitting a moral failure.

❑ I'll admit that I'm wrong just to end or avoid conflict so that we can be at peace. Who cares which of us is more at fault?

Leader Help

In order for group members to receive the maximum benefit from these questions and the following exercise, you may want to suggest that they request feedback from their spouses or close friends. An objective opinion on this issue can be invaluable, if the person is willing to receive it.

Perhaps you have been dodging some difficult truths. You know the wrong that stands between you and your child. You know you're responsible for some, if not all of it, yet you choose to pretend it doesn't exist. The truths feel as though they will overwhelm you with feelings and perspectives you cannot bear. Unfortunately, the solution you have chosen will not work forever. The longer you wait, the greater the distance grows.

—*Parenting: From Surviving to Thriving*

If a child cannot find resolution for pain or an injustice caused by his or her parent, how do you think that will affect his or her attitude toward the parent?

 ## DISCOVERING THE WAY

We discovered in lesson five that disconnected and damaged relationships at home produce dysfunctional family members; passive and permissive parents produce angry, frustrated children; and unresolved conflicts inflict wounds that never quite heal. All of these conditions existed for Absalom at the end of 2 Samuel 13. As we trace his descent from resentment to rebellion, our focus must remain on David. He is the central figure in the story and the parent from whom we can learn. As we noted in the previous lesson, we honor this great man by learning from his mistakes and avoiding them.

David's offense against Absalom was his passivity, his failure to give Absalom's beloved sister justice after Amnon brutally raped her. Unfortunately, the great king continued to be passive. Having failed Absalom (and Tamar) so miserably, he put off taking responsibility for his transgression.

Second Samuel 14 opens with the statement, "The king's heart was inclined toward Absalom." Yet David did nothing to reconnect with him. Verses 1–20 tell of how Joab, King David's general, convinced David to bring Absalom home. His elaborate scheme forced David's hand so that he had little choice but to bring the young man home. Only then did David act—and then only halfheartedly.

Read 2 Samuel 14:21 and 24. In what way is David's response confusing? Why do you think David did this?

According to 2 Samuel 13:38 and 14:28, how long did Absalom wait to see his father? What do you think was going on in the heart of David during that time? In the heart of Absalom? (Note 14:27.)

Skim through the story in 2 Samuel 14. Which of David's actions toward Absalom show evidence of controlling behavior or manipulation?

Leader Help

Some group members may feel as though we are picking on David or perhaps we are too critical of him. This feeling may distract them from gleaning all they can from his experience. Address the issue directly, invite the comments of those who might feel uncomfortable, and reassure them of the positive intentions of this lesson.

Second Samuel 14:33 describes the encounter between David and Absalom, the son he had not seen for five years. Read of the prodigal son's return in Luke 15:20–24. In the space below, compare and contrast the two reunions. How would you compare the kisses of the two fathers?

Children will never stop seeking the love of their parents until their parents prove that it cannot be had. David's superficial kiss confirmed what Absalom had suspected.

—*Parenting: From Surviving to Thriving*

After David and Absalom met and only superficially reconciled, the very next chapter describes the long-watered seeds of resentment sprouting into rebellion in the young man's heart. The encounter marks a significant turning point in Absalom's attitude toward David.

 Read 2 Samuel 14:30–32 and 2 Samuel 15:6. How had Absalom's attitude toward his father changed?

Beside each of the following verse references, describe Absalom's escalating actions toward his father.

2 Samuel 15:6

2 Samuel 15:10

2 Samuel 16:21–22

How would you describe David's attitude toward his son in 2 Samuel 18:5?

According to 2 Samuel 18:5 and 18:12, David wanted Absalom taken alive and treated well. Why do you think this was so important to him?

At first, David showed Absalom little compassion. Why do you think David's attitude toward his son changed so dramatically?

I can see David stopping for one last look at the city before leaving, perhaps forever. I imagine the unvarnished truth about how he came to be exiled by his own son came into clear focus. We see a different David after this moment. No more passivity, no more pride, only vulnerability. His heart had become contrite for his wrongdoing and grew tender toward Absalom.

—*Parenting: From Surviving to Thriving*

GETTING TO THE ROOT

In 2 Samuel 18:33, when David received the news that his son Absalom had been killed in battle, he "was deeply moved." This expression can be translated literally from the Hebrew as "he shook" or "he trembled." An accomplished storyteller paints word pictures in the reader's mind rather than merely telling us what happened. Here, the author could have written simply, "David was sad." Instead, he allowed us to experience the terrible anguish of a parent suffering the loss of his child and feeling largely responsible for his son's tragic end.

Upon hearing that Absalom had been killed, David trembled with grief. He staggered to a private room nearby, groaning with an anguish any parent can appreciate. "O my son Absalom! My son, my son Absalom! If only I had died instead of you—O Absalom, my son, my son!" (2 Samuel 18:33 NIV)

David had a long history of passivity and neglect in his relationships despite his many accomplishments elsewhere. Unparalleled as a king and a prodigy as a leader, he was a master on the battlefield, in the boardroom, and on the construction site. He was a musician, a poet, a prophet, and best of all, a supreme lover of God (1 Samuel 13:14). Nevertheless, David displayed little ability to enter the untidy, confusing world of intimate connection. He failed to see the need for resolution after conflict, the absolute necessity of his fatherly intervention in the face of rebellion, and even the subtle corroding effect of silence in relationships when something must be said. And in allowing Absalom to return to Jerusalem, he made a very common mistake: confusing proximity for closeness.

 STARTING YOUR JOURNEY

The story of David's passivity and neglect in the realm of family relationships serves to illustrate three principles that should prompt us to action and guide our steps. These will help keep all of our relationships free of clutter, but they are especially important for the parent. Because children are not equipped to take the initiative, we must. Determine how you will use these principles to repair your relationships or to keep them healthy.

1. Fractured relationships begin to heal when we're willing to hear and admit the truth.

Relationships are built on truth. We are foolish to think that we hold all or even most of that truth ourselves. That's why communication is essential when we experience conflict. Because our natural self-protective response is to recoil from potential pain, responding with silence, distance, or even control may feel like the best option. Until we are willing to drop our guard and open ourselves to truth, the relationship can't begin to be restored.

Describe the last time you feel reasonably sure you offended your child.

What have you done to resolve it? Or, if you have yet to do anything, what keeps you from addressing the wrong?

2. Reconciliation continues when we stop trying to control or manipulate the other person.

Control and *manipulation* are such emotionally charged words, they sound too sinister to be the work of normal, well-adjusted people. However, most of us tend

Anger doesn't become resentment overnight; it's a process that takes time. So does repairing a relationship. Reconciliation rarely occurs suddenly and completely all at once. Usually, it begins with a breakthrough and then grows as the two people learn to trust each other again. Typically, the longer the estrangement, the longer the time for complete restoration.

—*Parenting: From Surviving to Thriving*

to employ these very common self-defense mechanisms, especially in situations in which the other person cannot hold us accountable, such as with one of our children.

How willing are you to listen to your child's perspective on how you have offended him or her? Choose the response closest to how you feel, or write your own.

- ❑ I am deeply interested to know how he or she feels. I care very much to know if my child is hurting because of something I have said or done.

- ❑ His or her behavior has been so inexcusable, I don't really care to hear anything until I receive a proper apology.

- ❑ I feel so frustrated that my child doesn't understand what's really going on. If only he or she would hear me out.

- ❑ I am willing to listen, but I need my child to see his or her part in this.

- ❑ This situation is so confusing; I don't think anything good would come from talking about it.

- ❑ I know that I have a lot of ownership in this mess, but I can't bear to hear about it.

The crucial test for control or manipulation is how and whether or not you are communicating. Speaking or listening for any reason other than mutual understanding is likely a form of control. In this self-protective, self-justifying mode, words become weapons, and listening is just an opportunity for finding fault.

When we control or manipulate the relationship,

whether by blame or some other means, we remove God as the mediator. That puts us in charge—a very dangerous situation for everyone.

3. Final relief comes when we release all the resentment and take ownership of our responsibility.

The only remaining obstacle in our path is to release our grip on any resentment or claims of innocence. Failure to do this inevitably prolongs the pain and keeps us rehashing those imaginary arguments. In the end, we remain trapped in an endless cycle of self-justification, and we forfeit precious time enjoying our children. We will have exchanged joy for a mediocre life—and for what? The illusion of being right.

List at least one good reason to delay addressing an offense against your child. Then share the offense and your reason for delay with an impartial friend for his or her perspective.

When and how do you plan to address the wrong? What steps will you take to broach the subject with your child? Be specific.

Leader Help

This lesson would be a good opportunity to include some support. Divide group members into groups of three (same gender only) and have them exchange contact information. Allow each person to share his or her answers to the following questions with his or her accountability partners. Encourage the members to follow up with one another during the week and when they meet again.

Anger doesn't turn into resentment overnight; it takes time. So does repairing a relationship. Restoration of emotional closeness rarely occurs suddenly. Usually, it begins with a breakthrough and then grows as each person offers the other trust and affection. Typically, the longer the estrangement, the longer the time before complete restoration can be achieved.

Be patient. Be vulnerable. Be consistent. The Lord will honor your efforts however your relationship with your children turns out.

Lesson Seven

Affirming and Encouraging Words to Parents

— Luke 15:11–24 —

THE HEART OF THE MATTER

In Jesus's parable of the prodigal son, we find a very involved parent who refuses to control or squelch his sons, instead granting them as much freedom as possible to learn and grow. This father desires godly maturity and offers his influence, but he patiently waits for the Lord to change his children. Furthermore, and perhaps most important of all, his love is steeped in grace. All parents would do well to emulate this example of a godly father. He is, after all, patterned after our heavenly Father.

To prepare for this lesson, read Luke 15:11–24 and chapter 7 in *Parenting: From Surviving to Thriving*.

YOU ARE HERE

Parents often have a difficult time watching their children struggle with the lessons of life. We would love nothing more than to push aside the harsh schoolmasters of heartache and sorrow, so that we might offer a more gentle education. But if our children are determined not to listen, we can't teach them. Our patient instruction and guidance often turns into nagging, haranguing, control, manipulation, harsh-

By the end of this lesson, group members should recognize four commendable attitudes present in the prodigal son's father, aspire to allow their children increasing freedom as they mature, and prepare to respond with grace to their children's foolish choices.

85

ness, and even resentment. If we're not careful, we can find ourselves saying and doing the very things that caused us distress as children. As parents, we can change our attitude and our actions to create an environment in which our children can grow (and fail) as they mature.

Leader Help

As an encouragement to the group members, ask your pastor or another respected member of the community to write or record the answer to this question. Then share it with the group as you begin the session.

 Describe a time when you learned a valuable lesson the hard way. How does it affect your thinking and decision making today?

Did someone attempt to intervene in your difficult situation or convince you to choose differently? How did you respond?

The father created a comfortable, nurturing, grace-filled environment. I believe this to be one of the most important contributions a parent can make in a child's life. Words and actions are important, but the atmosphere we create has a huge impact on a child's sense of security and well-being.

—*Parenting: From Surviving to Thriving*

If your child were to face a very similar situation, what would you do?

 DISCOVERING THE WAY

In lessons five and six, we examined the family life of a very flawed father in the person of King David. Despite his many wonderful qualities as a king and as a man after God's own heart, he never embraced his role as father, leaving his children to rear themselves—with devastating results. David's sons were extremely difficult young men, but his passivity and distance as a father made a very difficult situation disastrous.

In contrast, we'll now investigate how a godly parent should guide a child, no matter how stubborn or rebellious the child may be. While the story Jesus told in Luke 15:11–24 is commonly known as the parable of the prodigal son, the father is the central and most important character. Strictly speaking, he's fictional—an imaginary character in a parable of Jesus. Yet he's also the most "real" father of all. In telling this story, Jesus revealed the parenting skills of his own Father. And by this example, we learn four essential attitudes that make for godly parenting.

 According to Luke 15:12, what did the father say or do in response to his son's impudent request?

Did the father argue or offer any resistance? Why do you think he handled the situation this way?

Leader Help

As you begin this section, have the group members brainstorm a modern-day example of the prodigal son's foolishness. This could be imaginary or an actual case. Write or draw it on a poster board or dry-erase board and keep it visible as you observe the story of the rebellious son and his grace-giving father.

On behalf of your children who have never used the word—and probably never will—you are their *hero*, Mom and Dad. Despite how ordinary or how inadequate you feel, you are a person of great courage, possessing noble qualities, someone working to achieve something great: turning children into healthy adults. You are to be commended for taking on this terribly difficult and largely thankless task.

—*Parenting: From Surviving to Thriving*

Unfortunately, when a child makes a mess of his or her life, the parents suffer as well—emotionally and often in other more tangible ways. In Jesus's parable, *the father was willing to listen to his son and allow him to make his own mistakes.* That kind of risk is necessary in order to permit young people to learn and grow.

 Because the father offered no resistance to his son's foolish plan, should we assume he didn't care? If not, what other explanation would you offer?

The young man was obviously "of age" and was determined to leave home. If the father had denied his request and compelled him to stay, how do you think it would have affected their relationship?

The father demonstrated that he was willing to release his son completely. Releasing a child is something parents practice well in advance of the day he or she leaves for college, the military, a marriage, or a job. Releasing a child begins the day he or she goes off to kindergarten and occurs each time the parent says yes to a request.

Read Luke 15:13–16. What happened to the young man's money? According to verse 16, who was there to help him when he was at his lowest point?

GETTING TO THE ROOT

Soon after leaving home, the foolish son began to engage in "loose living" (Luke 15:13). The Greek expression doesn't suggest that the young man had been engaged in evil or morally reprehensible behavior; he was merely foolish and wasteful. The term translated "loose living" means "dissipation." In naming the story, English translators chose the term *prodigal*, which means "recklessly extravagant, characterized by wasteful expenditure, lavish."[1] This is in perfect keeping with the Greek term. The respected *Theological Dictionary of the New Testament* reads, "[Luke] 15:13 speaks of the dissipated life of the Prodigal without specifying the nature of this life . . . . It is simply depicted as carefree and spendthrift in contrast to the approaching [famine]."[2] In other words, we are not told how he blew his fortune, only that it was gone because he was foolish.

The father certainly would have heard news about the famine. Why wouldn't he have checked on his son? Why do you think he did not go after his son or invite him home?

The father's absence might seem callous to some. Instead, the father wisely left his son to wallow in the pigsty of his consequences. As personally painful as the experience was for the father, he was willing to wait for God to change his son's heart instead of manipulating or browbeating him. A mark of maturity is the ability to think and make wise decisions for one's self. Unfortunately, this requires personal experience. And personal experience requires the opportunity to fail.

We provide the opportunity to fail in two important ways. First, *we grant our child freedom to risk.* We offer our counsel and warn of the likely consequences but allow our child to choose. Second, *we grant our child grace when he fails.* A scowling "I told you so!" only reinforces the message that risk and personal responsibility are to be avoided at all cost.

 In Luke 15:20, which verbs describe the father's reaction upon his son's return? (Most Bible versions list five.)

What do these actions reveal about the father's attitude toward his son's poor choices? Toward his son's decision to return? Toward the financial and emotional implications the father has endured?

In Luke 15:18–19, the son rehearsed a speech. Compare it to Luke 15:21. What prevented him from delivering the last part?

The young man returned to his father expecting no special treatment. In fact, he hoped for nothing more than a job as a household slave. His father, however, greeted him with three symbolic gifts: a robe, a ring, and a pair of shoes. The best robe was usually reserved for the father. In ancient times, a ring gave the wearer the authority to seal business deals and to make large purchases. It served much like a credit card today. Finally, the father completed his boy's restoration with a flourish— the unnecessary extravagance of sandals. All three gifts conferred upon the young man his former status as a son. This father's actions reveal a fourth attitude: *a willingness to receive, forgive, and restore his son.*

Based on your study of this story, what kind of parent is this father? Describe what he would be like if he were alive today.

What parallels can you draw between this father's actions and God's treatment of His children?

The boy was still caked with the stench and grime of the pigsty, still dripping with the sweat of his long walk home as his father placed a clean linen robe on him—the robe he normally reserved for himself. The father accepted his son as he was, forgave him freely, and restored him completely. Then he danced.

—*Parenting: From Surviving to Thriving*

STARTING YOUR JOURNEY

In our study of Luke 15:11–24, we discovered a father who possessed at least four constructive attitudes. He was willing to listen to his son and take risks in his development. He was willing to release his son rather than control him. He was willing to wait for God to change his son's heart instead of manipulating or browbeating him. And he was willing to receive, forgive, and restore his son, even after the colossal mess the boy had made of his life.

We can learn to cultivate these attitudes in our parenting even if they don't come naturally. Very often, they follow a self-perpetuating pattern: choosing the appropriate action sparks the right attitude, which in turn makes wise action easier to choose.

Prayer is essential; only the work of Holy Spirit can change you . . . and your kids, for that matter. Whether your children are living in complete rebellion or are simply learning to make decisions on their own, you can do something in addition to praying. Follow the example of the father in Luke 15:11–24.

1. *Be willing to listen to your children and take risks in their development.*

Most people have a need to have their perspectives and opinions honored with a fair hearing. A child has an easier time considering the input of an authority figure when the child feels that all of the information, including the child's perspective, has been taken into account. Then demonstrate a willingness to bend. Flexibility will actually increase the child's desire to discuss decisions with you and reduce the likelihood of outright disobedience.

 What privilege or activity have you denied your child recently that other reasonable parents seem to have no problem permitting?

What about the privilege or activity causes you to hesitate?

How much of this hesitation is legitimate parental concern and how much is your desire to avoid personal discomfort?

Parents can begin releasing their child responsibly over time by becoming "yes" parents. This is an internal commitment a parent makes to say yes to any request unless something *compels* a "no" answer. This will require a significant personal investment of time and effort. It almost always involves an element of risk, and it frequently involves money. Stretch yourself. Say yes. The dividends of this good-faith investment will be a relationship relatively free of rebellion and the development of a surprisingly responsible young man or woman.

2. *Be willing to surrender the entire matter to the Lord, which will allow you the freedom to release your child.*

 If you were to let go of any plans or expectations for the return of your child, what do you fear would happen?

The concept of surrender is very different from giving up. You're not simply letting the matter drop, deciding not to care; that's giving in to defeat. When you surren-

You see, "no" is the easy answer. It requires no thought, no effort, no expense, no risk, no anxiety, no trust, no growth, nothing. Furthermore, it's a sure way to build resentment into the relationship, which will likely turn into a perpetual game of tug-of-war, maybe even outright rebellion.

—*Parenting: From Surviving to Thriving*

der your child, you're releasing him or her to One greater than yourself and trusting—believing—that He is both willing and able to care for your child better than you ever could.

(For more help understanding the process of surrender, see Charles R. Swindoll, *So, You Want to Be Like Christ? Eight Essentials to Get You There* [Nashville: W Publishing Group, 2005], 79–98.)

3. Be willing to wait for the Lord to change your child without insisting that you help the process along.

 What heart change do you most wish for your child? What change in his or her thinking, feelings, or perspective do you most desire?

What have you done in the past to help bring about the change? How effective have your actions been?

Once you have done all you reasonably can, only three options remain: try unreasonable approaches (the choice of many parents), give up and stop caring, or place it before the Lord in prayer. God gave us prayer as an antidote to the poison of worry. Whenever the issue with your child comes to mind, turn it into an opportunity for prayer. Express your worry to Him. Submit your desires to Him. Ask Him for wisdom in how best to interact with your child regarding the issue.

4. *Be willing to receive, forgive, and restore your child.*

 When your child disappoints you or experiences a big failure, what do you think he or she fears most when facing you?

What can you do to relieve his or her anxiety right away?

When your child is genuinely repentant, how long does it usually take to replace your disappointment with an attitude of acceptance? What do you do to express your acceptance?

After a particularly serious breach of trust, healing will require time. Feelings of joy and closeness will not return right away. It isn't necessary to shield your child from the negative consequences of sin or poor choices. However, you can do something that expresses your acceptance of him or her and your desire for restoration in time. Affirm your love, affirm your dedication to the healing process, and express your confidence that the two of you will enjoy an increasingly close relationship in the future.

DIGGING DEEPER

In the spirit of turning your study toward practical application, consider three primary questions. Except in unusual circumstances, every parent must answer yes to each.

1. Do you have a parent you need to thank?

If you have had children for very long, you know the almost debilitating feelings of inadequacy and guilt that can weigh on a mom or dad. Ask many parents the question, "Were you a good parent?" and their minds immediately recall all the things they should have done that they didn't, all the mistakes they made, the wisdom they gained too late, and the innumerable regrets. They forget the successes. They overlook the security they provided, the messes they cleaned up, the sacrifices they made, the moments their children found so special that they may have never considered.

Your parents need to hear from you. They need to be affirmed in their value as parents. Your encouragement can go a long way.

2. Do you have a son or daughter you need to release?

Releasing a son or daughter is something parents must practice well in advance of the day the child leaves for college, the military, a marriage, or a job. The decision to release begins no later than the first day of kindergarten and presents itself each time your child asks, "Can I . . .?"

Parental instinct can be both our greatest asset and

Leader Help

Help group members apply the lessons in the "Digging Deeper" feature by making time for this interactive activity. Distribute thank-you cards, pens, envelopes, and stamps near the end of the session. Encourage members to write their mother, father, or other very important childhood influence a specific thank-you note. Then have them address the envelope and place a stamp on it for the next day's outgoing mail.

our child's greatest obstacle to personal growth. Very often, parents underestimate the maturity and decision-making capability of their child by drawing upon their past personal experiences. Unfortunately, studying our own childhood through the eyes of an adult will invariably cause us to be unreasonably conservative—for a variety of reasons.

And let's face it, we're tired! Sometimes—perhaps too often—we say no because yes adds another obligation to an already impossible day. Rather than admitting we're too overextended to allow our child a reasonable opportunity for fun or freedom, we'll conjure a reason to say no that feels legitimate. But children are smarter than we give them credit for. They know a ruse when they see one.

3. *Do you have a prodigal who needs forgiveness and restoration?*

By "a prodigal," we mean any child who has rejected, or is currently rejecting, your leadership in favor of a lifestyle contrary to his or her rearing. He or she may have left the home or may well be on the way to complete rebellion. We highly recommend two resources:

Tim Kimmel's book *Why Christian Kids Rebel: Trading Heartache for Hope* (Nashville: W Publishing Group, 2004) addresses the most common reasons children rebel. You will likely discover that you have greater influence than you realize, but the changes in your child may have to begin with yourself. Dr. Kimmel takes a gentle yet forthright approach to exploring the parent-child relationship and how the developing, adolescent mind interprets your words and actions.

John White wrote *Parents in Pain: Overcoming the Hurt and Frustration of Problem Children* (Downers Grove, IL: InterVarsity, 1979) to help struggling parents keep a balanced perspective. With great empathy and sensitivity, he coaches parents through the process of reestablishing an authentic, truthful relationship with their child. He helps parents uncover and take ownership of their mistakes without excusing their child's sinful choices.

Rearing children in grace is, without question, one of the most demanding jobs on earth. To fulfill the role successfully, we must be perpetual students of grace ourselves, for we cannot pass on what we do not possess. And let's face it, none of us is equal to the task alone. We need the continual transformation and instruction of Jesus Christ through the internal ministry of the Holy Spirit. We need constant refreshment and instruction from God's Word. And we need regular encouragement from fellow strugglers.

Parents need grace.

Be encouraged, good parent. You have a heavenly Father who understands your experience. At present count, He has roughly 6.5 billion prodigal children! And He longs to receive you, to nurture you, to prepare and equip you, and to fulfill your role as parent with you, through you, and for you.

(To learn more about how to have a relationship with your heavenly Father, read "How to Begin a Relationship with God" on page 177 of this workbook.)

Lesson Eight

Confronting the "Older Brother Attitudes"

— Luke 15:25–32 —

THE HEART OF THE MATTER

When Jesus told the story of the wasteful, foolish son who repented and returned to his father, He wanted to expose a prevalent attitude. When the repentant son received grace when he should have been turned away, the older son's response revealed a condemning, vengeful attitude. On the outside, the older brother appeared to be the responsible, loyal, "good" son who loved his father and faithfully tended his sheep. In fact, his heart could not have been more opposed to the values his father held.

In these three characters, we can discover valuable insight for family life in general and parenting in particular. Unfortunately, Pharisees are alive and well today, and if we look carefully, we'll discover one living much closer to us than we think. Their effect on the peace and health of a family can be profound, so we must do what we can to confront their "older brother attitudes" with gentleness and grace.

To prepare for this lesson, read Luke 15:25–32 and chapter 8 in *Parenting: From Surviving to Thriving*.

Leader Help

By the end of this lesson, group members should be able to identify with the main characters in the story of the prodigal son and recognize what kind of people each one represents; and they should commit to exercising the father's grace toward their family members, especially their children.

YOU ARE HERE

Along with death and taxes, we can count on at least one other certainty: family friction. As long as humans have a sinful nature and live in close quarters, occasional conflict will disrupt the peace and safety of home life. However, chronic or persistent tension between two or more members of a household is not a normal part of family life. Rather than chalk it up to differences in personality or accept it in the vain hope that it will resolve itself in time, we should directly address recurring conflict, especially if the issues involve foundational, deep-rooted ways of thinking.

Henri Nouwen described one particular malady of the soul that affects many homes and can make Christian families no less dysfunctional than their unbelieving neighbors.

Leader Help

In response to the questions that follow, some group members may desire to elaborate on the attitudes and behaviors of others in their family. Given the nature of this lesson, the best response would be to allow them some opportunity to vent their frustration and to offer a few words of empathy without further comment. "That must be very difficult to bear. I'm sorry you're having such a tough time. Perhaps we can talk more about it after the session."

Looking deeply into myself and then around me at the lives of other people, I wonder which does more damage, lust or resentment? There is so much resentment among the "just" and the "righteous." There is so much judgment, condemnation, and prejudice among the "saints." There is so much frozen anger among the people who are so concerned about avoiding "sin."

The lostness of the resentful "saint" is so hard to reach precisely because it is so closely wedded to the desire to be good and virtuous.[1]

The two people in our household who experience the
most acute conflict are:

Which of the following attitudes or behaviors do you see exhibited in your home?

❑ Attempting to control others	❑ Shame
❑ Arrogance	❑ Exaggerating the negative behavior of others.
❑ Unwillingness or resistance to being proven wrong	❑ Condemning others for decisions that have no clear moral implications
❑ Always having to be right	❑ Skepticism or condemnation of activities that have no purpose other than pleasure
❑ Accusing another of hidden intentions	❑ Maintaining a public image
❑ Focusing on external signs of righteousness rather than internal	❑ Performing to feel loved or accepted
❑ Looking for ways to be offended	❑ Seeming to enjoy being indignant
❑ Excessive need for the approval of church leaders or members	❑ A general attitude of disapproval
❑ Perfectionism	❑ Customarily feeling misunderstood or unappreciated.

In which of your family members do you see these attitudes or behaviors? Be honest.

Review the parable of the prodigal son in Luke 15:11–32, paying particular attention to verses 25–32. In the story of the prodigal son, with which character do you most identify?

Which family member would you identify with the older brother in the story?

Jesus's parable pictures two children receiving the love of their father in very different ways. From them, we can discover valuable insight for family life in general and parenting in particular. If we take care to notice, we'll inevitably discover a legalist living very close to us—perhaps in our own household.

DISCOVERING THE WAY

In the previous chapter, we examined the character of a rebellious son and his grace-filled father. Another son lived in the household—the "good" son. He was, by all accounts, morally right and steadfastly faithful to his father. However, rebellion need not be merely external. As one author writes about the older son in this parable,

> After all, he did all the right things. He was obedient, dutiful, law-abiding, and hardworking. People respected him, admired him, praised him, and likely considered him a model son. Outwardly, the elder son was faultless. But when confronted by his father's joy at the return of his younger brother, a dark power erupts in him and boils to the surface. Suddenly, there becomes glaringly visible a resentful, proud, unkind, selfish person, one that had remained deeply hidden, even though it had been growing stronger and more powerful over the years.[2]

It's no coincidence that Jesus told the story of the prodigal son in the context of a meal with "tax collectors and sinners" (Luke 15:1–2). The Pharisees were outside grumbling at the thought of socially intermixing with such lowlifes as Jesus's dinner companions. In response to this situation, Jesus's story of two brothers—who could not have been more different—addressed two kinds of people within the His society (and ours). The first group, represented by the younger son, consisted of people who were systematically shunned by the religious elite. Tax collectors were universally hated by the Jewish community

Anyone with brothers and/or sisters can appreciate the almost primal emotions involved in sibling conflict. Irritating behavior by someone outside the family may draw frustration, while the same actions by a family member can inspire deep resentment or even hatred. As parents, we can't afford to take persistent negative attitudes or menacing resentments between siblings lightly.

—*Parenting: From Surviving to Thriving*

because they became the quisling puppets of the oppressive Roman Empire. Their self-serving choice was not unlike that of the Jews who cooperated with Hitler's persecution during the Nazi holocaust of the 1940s, betraying their brothers to better their own situation.

Pharisees, represented by the older brother, wouldn't let as much as let the hem of their robes touch tax collectors, to say nothing of treating them kindly or sharing a meal with them. The daily passion of the Pharisees was the pursuit of righteousness, or moral correctness. To accomplish this, they created a detailed list of what they believed to be God's desired behaviors and then put all of their energies into keeping the list perfectly. Naturally, when Jesus called Matthew, a tax collector, to be His disciple and when He dined with people whom they considered the very worst of sinners, the Pharisees could barely contain their rage (see Matthew 9:9–13). Jesus's parable addressed their attitudes of moral superiority and resistance to grace in the character of the older brother.

> Legalists cannot see anything beyond themselves. They only pretend to value what God values by pretending to love righteousness. But if their hearts truly beat with His, they would join the party when the unrighteous repent.
>
> —*Parenting: From Surviving to Thriving*

 According to Luke 15:25–26, why didn't the older brother already know about his brother's return and the ensuing celebration?

Based on his speech in verses 29–30, why did he become angry?

Leader Help

Encourage group members to empathize with the older brother and to view him with compassion. Play "devil's advocate" if you must in order to argue on behalf of the older brother. (Be sure, of course, to let the group members know that this is what you're doing.)

Did he make a good point? Why or why not?

In verse 30, the older brother alleged that his brother squandered his inheritance on prostitutes. Nothing in Luke 15:11–24 mentions this detail. Why would he say this?

In Luke 15:30, what words did the older son use to refer to his brother? Why do you think he did this?

Based on the above, what words or image would you use to describe the older brother's attitude?

Despite [the father's] gentle reasoning, the self-righteous son clung to his resentment, something that Alcoholics Anonymous says is like drinking poison and expecting the other person to die. And from his point of view, he had good reason. With the prodigal wallowing in a pigsty, the older brother looked like a saint. Against his brother's waste and avarice, the legalist's own loyalty and conscientiousness looked superhuman. And with his rival off in a distant land, he could bask in the glow of his father's undivided attention.

—*Parenting: From Surviving to Thriving*

DOORWAY TO HISTORY

In reasoning with his bitter older son, the father reminded him, "All that is mine is yours" (Luke 15:31). According to Jewish law, a father was to distribute the family wealth evenly among his sons, with one exception. The eldest male was to receive a double portion of the estate. But the "right of the firstborn" involved more than money. In patriarchal societies, families maintained a close association under the authority of an elder male, who served much like a king. When the eldest son received the blessing from his father, he received the reins of leadership of the clan (see Genesis 27:27–29). From that day on, he was responsible for their safety and prosperity, as well as for deciding matters of justice. Furthermore, he was responsible for carrying out priestly duties on behalf of the family.[3]

In Jesus's story, the father took an early retirement, gave the younger son his one-third portion, and transferred the rest to the older brother. Not only did the older son receive his father's material wealth, but he also received his father's rights, privileges, priestly duties, and authority!

In Luke 15:29, the older son recalled his good works. What did he expect in return? How does their value compare to what the father said the older son already had in verse 31?

In verse 30, the older son recalled his brother's failure and the reward he received. Why was he so astonished?

From the older brother's perspective, what is the relationship between righteousness and blessing?

This father's love is not altered encountering this boy. He showed the older son the same gentle grace he gave the younger. He even acknowledged his "faithfulness" and showed him appreciation. Yet the older brother's attitude would not allow him to experience his father's grace. His desire to make himself worthy of the father's love *in his own eyes* prevented him from seeing his need for it, and so he failed to receive the love had had been given all along.

What about from the father's perspective?

—*Parenting: From Surviving to Thriving*

The older brother's primary concern was fairness, the proper balance of justice as he understood it. According to Luke 15:32, what was the father's primary concern?

The father in Jesus's parable was secure enough to release his fleeing boy without an argument. He was strong enough to patiently wait for his return. He was faithful enough to keep praying and watching despite the lack of visible hope. He was forgiving enough to receive his son without browbeating or lecturing upon his return. He was generous enough to restore his boy to his former place of honor, despite how little he deserved it. He was gracious enough to plead for the older son's humility. Grace saturated his every word and deed, yet he never lowered his standards or set aside his love for righteousness. For the father, unlike the older brother, grace and righteousness were not mortal enemies.

Leader Help

The conversation may get lively at this point. Be on the lookout for denial! However, remind the group members to season their comments with love. Few people learn very much when put on the defensive.

 ## STARTING YOUR JOURNEY

How true do the following statements seem to you? Circle one.

When good things happen to me, it indicates God's interest in and good pleasure with me.

Not at all   A little   Somewhat   Mostly   Always
|————————|————————|————————|————————|————————|

When bad things happen to me, it's probably because I did something wrong.

Not at all   A little   Somewhat   Mostly   Always
|————————|————————|————————|————————|————————|

How do you think the older brother in Jesus's story would have answered these two questions?

What do your marks above say about your understanding of grace and how your heavenly Father thinks about you?

In the "You Are Here" section, we considered some negative, family-disrupting attitudes and behaviors. How much effort did you put into examining yourself?

Whom did you name as the "older brother"?

With which character did you most identify?

How seriously have you considered the possibility that you might have much in common with the older brother—that you might have a "Pharisee" living within you?

The weakness of a soul is proportionate to the number of truths that must be kept from it.

—*Eric Hoffer*[4]

If you are like most people, you will find more of the "older brother" lurking within you than you realized. And in truth, one of your family members may be, indeed, the very personification of legalism. Nevertheless, wherever we encounter these "older brother attitudes"—within ourselves or others—we must confront them not with condemnation and rejection but with the same gentle grace as the father in Luke 15:25–32. He praised the pharisaical son for his earnest faithfulness; he reaffirmed his love for the older son; he begged the older son to join the family in celebration; and he illustrated grace in his final words, "We had to celebrate and rejoice, for this brother of yours was dead and has begun to live, and was lost and has been found" (15:32). In other words, he spoke and lived the truth in love.

How can you confront your own "older brother attitudes" and behavior with gentleness and grace?

Following the father's example in Jesus's story, how can you respond to any other "Pharisees" in your family with gentleness and grace?

The story of the prodigal son involves a mischievous paradox. If, at the end of the story, we find ourselves condemning the Pharisee, we ourselves have become the older brother to the older brother! Each of us must admit that, at least to some degree, a Pharisee lives within. The "older brother attitude" we must confront first is our own. And we must confront ourselves with the same gentleness and grace the Father demonstrates. When we can embrace the Pharisee within, we are ready to confront the "older brother attitudes" we encounter in others.

Lesson Nine

Increasing the Priority of Your Family

— Psalms 127 and 128 —

THE HEART OF THE MATTER

A sound, stable household cannot be established and maintained on human effort alone. Love and worship of the Lord must permeate the family, and the parents must treasure their children as gifts. When priority is given to the family over career and personal fulfillment, parents will receive blessings that strengthen future generations and preserve peace in their community.

To prepare for this lesson, read Psalms 127 and 128, and chapter 9 in *Parenting: From Surviving to Thriving*.

YOU ARE HERE

During the 1990s, Vice President Dan Quayle commented on the decline of traditional family values and cited a popular television show as an example of how media contributes to the downward trend. An eight-second sound bite from his speech sparked a national debate on the definition and purpose of the family. The intensity of the dispute clearly indicated that something significant had changed. The question "What is a family?" begged a

---

Leader Help

By the end of this lesson, group members should recognize the futility of trying to establish a thriving household apart from the Lord and commit to giving Him first priority in the home. They should also acknowledge that each child is a gift from the Lord to be treasured and that a strong family strengthens a community. Each group member should also commit to giving his or her family priority over career or personal fulfillment.

second: "What is the purpose of a family?" As a result, a sad fact became clear. Many were not quite sure.

Based on your best guess or by doing a little research, list the five most-watched television programs that feature a family or a group of people who consider themselves a family. Indicate whether or not the roles of father, mother, or child are represented in the primary home.

Leader Help

Check your television listings for the top-rated shows featuring a family or a group of people who consider themselves a family. Select the top five and prepare a poster board to display either pictures or names of the programs. Leave enough room beneath them to record responses to the questions that follow.

Program Title	Father	Mother	Children
1.	❑	❑	❑
2.	❑	❑	❑
3.	❑	❑	❑
4.	❑	❑	❑
5.	❑	❑	❑

Which program in current production most conforms to your concept of the best family structure?

Reflecting on the program with which you are most familiar, what are the top three priorities of the parents? Where would you say the children rank?

Do the parental figures on these programs nurture and support the children? How?

Reflecting on life in the real world, what do you think should be the father's primary responsibility in the family? What do you think should be the mother's?

If your family were to adopt the priorities modeled in the television show, what might be some of the implications (comic and/or tragic)?

In our highly efficient, pragmatic culture, we too often settle for the bare minimum when it comes to family life. As long as a household has a father and a mother who remain married and who faithfully feed, shelter, and clothe their children, we consider it a strong household, a family worth emulating. But according to the Bible, that's merely a good beginning. The Lord desires much more for His people and the community in which they live.

The quantity and quality of your memories are the measure of a life well lived, and they are built upon moments in time shared with those you love—time spent *with* them, not tasks done *for* them.

—*Parenting: From Surviving to Thriving*

Now let's be honest. How connected are we to the other people living under our roof? If it weren't for cell phones and text messaging, how much contact would you have with your children? When was the last time you spent a solid thirty minutes deliberately nurturing someone bearing your genes?

—*Parenting: From Surviving to Thriving*

DISCOVERING THE WAY

Research has demonstrated an unmistakable correlation between the strength of the family and the strength of the culture in which it exists. Like the teeth of one gear mesh with that of another, the attitudes that undermine a family will ultimately bring down a nation.[1] Unfortunately, developments during the last couple of decades indicate that the priority of family is on the decline.

As Christian parents, we have an opportunity to do what we can to halt the downward slide and perhaps even reverse the trend in our communities. The place to start is within our own families. And the principles and reminders found in Psalms 127 and 128 give us every reason for hope.

Many Bible expositors call Psalms 120–134 "The Little Psalter." The ancient editors of the Hebrew Scriptures compiled these fifteen short psalms and labeled each "A Song of the Ascents." No one knows for certain why they are called ascent psalms; however, the most credible theory holds that Hebrew worshipers sang them as they climbed the fifteen steps leading to the temple. Faithful Jews visited the temple during each of Israel's three annual festivals and ascended the stairs, pausing on each step to recite or sing the corresponding psalm. Most of the ascent psalms are very short and reflect upon almost every important facet of life in the Jewish community. Not surprisingly, the middle two, Psalms 127 and 128, contemplate the Lord's relationship with the family and how important healthy, God-honoring families are to the prosperity of the nation.

Builders can construct a palatial house, but if the Lord isn't crafting the family inside, every square foot is wasted space.

—*Parenting: From Surviving to Thriving*

[1]Unless the LORD builds the house,
   They labor in vain who build it;
   Unless the LORD guards the city,
   The watchman keeps awake in vain.
[2]It is vain for you to rise up early,
   To retire late,
   To eat the bread of painful labors;
   For He gives to His beloved even in his sleep.
   (Psalm 127:1–2)

 What phrase appears twice in Psalm 127:1?

What word is used three times in Psalm 127:1–2?

According to these verses, who is responsible for building a house and keeping it safe?

Leader Help
Because the following questions require close observation of specific words in the text, we have inserted the New American Standard Bible translation of the passage. Encourage the group members to observe the text in other versions as well.

DOORWAY TO HISTORY

Unless the LORD builds the house,
They labor in vain who build it. (Psalm 127:1)

The Old Testament doesn't have a specific word that describes what we think of today as a family: a father and a mother rearing their children under a single roof. Sociologists call this modern, Western arrangement the "nuclear family"; it was made necessary by the industrial revolution of the late nineteenth and early twentieth centuries. A relatively recent development, this family structure would have been unfamiliar to the ancient Hebrew. For many thousands of years, the "extended family" ruled. According to Alvin Toffler:

> Before the industrial revolution . . . family forms varied from place to place. But wherever agriculture held sway, people tended to live in large, multigenerational households, with uncles, aunts, in-laws, grandparents, or cousins all living under the same roof, all working together as an economic production unit. . . . And the family was immobile—rooted to the soil.[2]

This description is similar to what the ancient Hebrew knew as a "house" or "household" (*bayit*). The term encompassed more than a building and even more than the people living in it. "House" referred to the family's name, legacy, identity, and participation in the community. Furthermore, a house functioned very much like a small kingdom, providing sustenance and protection to everyone bearing the family name, including servants.

Psalm 127:2 seems to suggest that the Lord considers hard work to be futile. However, we know from Proverbs 6:6–11 that the Lord honors hard work and He considers laziness the mark of a fool. What point do you think the psalmist is trying to make in verse 2?

If we have genuine confidence that the Lord—and not our (or our spouse's) vocation—will feed and protect our family, in what ways will our priorities change?

Based on our study of Psalm 127:1–2, we can derive two interrelated principles. We'll discover a third in the next section.

1. *It is futile to build a home or a family using only human effort.*

2. *The Lord must have first priority over everything, including the home and the family.*

The temptation is to think that if we work hard enough, apply enough education, or put in long enough hours, we can eventually get far enough ahead to cut back later. But thinking anything will ever be enough is the self-delusion of the work-obsessed, sacrificing a thousand sunny days for that one potential rainy day. . . . Their temptation is to add hours to their day and days to their weeks, to rise early and go to bed late, to choke down fast food on the way from one task to another, to feel satisfied with the spoils of hard labor.

—*Parenting: From Surviving to Thriving*

³Behold, children are a gift of the LORD,
  The fruit of the womb is a reward.
⁴Like arrows in the hand of a warrior,
  So are the children of one's youth.
⁵How blessed is the man whose quiver is full of them.
  (Psalm 127:3–5)

The last line of Psalm 127:2 reveals that the Lord builds a house by giving to his beloved. What do verses 3–4 say are His gifts to a household?

From this perspective, what is the greatest asset to the health and strength of a family?

Psalm 127:4 likens children to arrows in a warrior's hand. At the time when the psalmist drew this word picture, battles were usually fought in close quarters, hand to hand, using swords, clubs, and spears. Imagine the advantage a warrior would have if he could stand at a safe distance and fire arrows at his enemies. With a full quiver, he could defeat them and win the battle without ever risking his life. Arrows were very valuable indeed!

In fact, carrying the metaphor further in verse 5, the psalmist goes on to say, "How happy is the man whose quiver is full of them!" (NLT). This carries the idea of "blessed many times over." Children are not a burden or just mouths to feed. Whether you planned for them or not, they are entrusted to you by God and given as a blessing.

GETTING TO THE ROOT

The psalmist chose an unusual word to describe the value of children in Psalm 127:2. The term usually rendered "reward" is *sakar*, which means, literally, "wages." The verb form of this noun means "to hire."

We don't typically think of children as a paycheck, but the Lord directed the psalmist to use a bit of irony to shift our paradigm. He says, in effect, "Don't work yourself to the bone to supply your family's needs; that's My responsibility. Instead of laboring for a larger salary, labor for Me, and I will reward you with children you can be proud of."

Children are both a gift from God and a household's greatest asset. How does this knowledge affect your view of your vocation?

Many parents try to rationalize the lack of adequate time invested in their children by suggesting that the precious moments they do spend are meaningful. Unfortunately, the "quality time" myth reinforces the notion that mothers and fathers can pursue personal fulfillment at no expense to the home or the well-being of their children. If we're honest with ourselves, we must admit that we all struggle with this temptation. We are by nature, by birth, and by choice sinful, selfish creatures. We too easily become work-obsessed because we trust our paycheck more than the Lord and because our vocation gives us personal fulfillment. We may try to mask our vocational goals as "sacrifice" or "provision," but this deceives neither our children nor the Lord.

Our study of Psalm 127:3–5 brings us to a third principle:

3. Each child is to be treasured as God's gift and given priority over our vocations.

Each child is to be cherished and given more time and attention than we devote to our career or pursuits that bring us personal fulfillment. If we faithfully do this, we can expect a marvelous mutual benefit. According to verse 5, we will be blessed and our child will gain confidence and position within the community.

According to Psalm 127:5, children who are given priority by their parents will represent the family in the community and will not be ashamed. Why do think this is true?

Psalm 128 opens with the same words that closed Psalm 127: "How blessed!" It paints a vivid picture of a family that maintains excellent priorities. To illustrate how Psalm 128 fulfills the principles found in Psalm 127, read the verses of the two songs in the following order:

Psalm 127:1
Psalm 128:1
Psalm 127:2–3
Psalm 128:2–3
Psalm 127:4
Psalm 128:4
Psalm 127:5
Psalm 128:5–6

Psalm 128 concludes with the blessing, "Shalom to Israel!" *Shalom* means much more than "peace." It also includes the ideas of prosperity, completeness, safety, health, security, and friendship. To bid someone *shalom* is to wish upon them the greatest possible state of well-being. When we enjoy the wonders of heaven, we will experience the full meaning of *shalom*.

As parents, our responsibility and greatest joy is to give our children priority over career, personal fulfillment, or any other endeavor (except our relationship with God and our marriage). If we will, blessings from the Lord will flood our household with joy and spill over to our neighborhood.

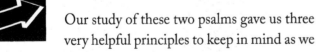

STARTING YOUR JOURNEY

Our study of these two psalms gave us three very helpful principles to keep in mind as we elevate the priority of our families. Putting them into action, then, becomes our challenge. Very often, we can hold certain values and priorities in our hearts yet fail to translate them into real life. How do we increase the priority of family on a day-to-day basis? Perhaps four simple

Leader Help

This set of questions can easily lead group members to offer answers that would please others rather than to explore their true feelings and evaluate their current circumstances. For example, in some cases, a parent *should* sacrifice time with the family in the interest of providing for them. However, it should be a conscious decision for a limited time and for a specific purpose. Encourage the group members to seek the honest truth of their individual situations.

reminders will help. These reminders are simple to state and difficult to execute, but they are worth the effort.

1. *Think family.*

Before you move, before you accept the promotion, before you commit yourself to the big project or the tight deadline, think family.

What responsibilities or commitments have demanded time and energy from you lately?

Which will do your spouse and children the greater good: the financial benefits of your career advancement or the time and energy invested with your family?

Share your answer with your spouse or with a trusted, mature friend, and ask him or her to give an honest critique of your priorities.

At the end of your life, you will never regret not having passed one more test, not winning one more verdict or not closing one more deal. You will regret time not spent with a husband, a child, a friend or a parent.... Your success as a family ... our success as a society depends not on what happens in the White House, but on what happens inside your house.[3]

—*Barbara Bush*

If freeing yourself up to spend more time with your family meant moving to a smaller home or trading down to a less expensive car, how do you think your family would respond?

Ask each of them individually and record what you discover in the space below.

2. *Say no.*

No quite possibly can be the most powerful and liberating word you can add to your vocabulary. Unfortunately, two difficult issues make this a rare word on the lips of many parents: people-pleasing and the fear of being rude.

 When approached to take on an added responsibility or commitment, to whom do you have the most difficulty saying no?

What do you most fear will happen?

How do you think your family would react if it did?

What do you think God's take is on the matter?

Whose opinion means most to you?

3. *Take time.*

The purpose of saying no to competing priorities is to say yes to your family. Turn off the television. Do a project together. Play together. Take a walk, ask some questions, discuss issues, discover one another's hopes, fears, favorite color, or fondest memory. Get out of the house and do something unusual, or if you rarely have time at home together, plan a quiet evening in.

When you are together, try asking an open-ended question. Choose from the list below or think of one on your own. As your child shares, actively listen and ask follow-up questions. See how long you can keep him or her talking. You will likely discover much more than you imagined, which will deepen your knowledge and strengthen your bond.

Questions for Younger Children

- Who is your best friend? Why do you like him/her so much?

- Who is your favorite teacher? Why?

- Who is your meanest teacher? What does he/she do that makes him/her mean?

- What subject is the easiest for you?

- Who do you most want to be like?

Questions for Older Children

- What do you fear more than anything in the world? Why?

- If you could live anywhere on earth, where would you live? Why there?

- If you could have one fully developed talent instantly, what would it be?

- What subject in school gives you the most difficulty? Why? Which do you prefer? Why?

- Who is your favorite entertainer? Why?

4. *Be patient.*

No one builds a house in a single day. Begin slowly; give your family time to adjust to the change in pattern. You might start by attending their games, plays, band performances, or other activities. Work up to taking a child to dinner, just the two of you, or with your mate. Then perhaps you can plan all-day outings or play dates where you do something fun together.

When parents increase the priority of their families, everyone benefits. The Lord receives honor. The children enjoy security and discover their worth. Parents find lasting fulfillment that carries on long past retirement. And the community is strengthened by the influence of citizens who want to add to rather than subtract from the public good.

Like anything worthwhile, placing family above vocation or personal fulfillment is an investment—a sacrifice for the sake of greater returns.

Lesson Ten

Restoring Relationships After You've Blown It

— Isaiah 58:1–12 —

THE HEART OF THE MATTER

Because we are human and we live in a fallen world, we have all experienced the pain of broken relationships. As we commit ourselves to the process of reconciliation, we must keep in mind three important truths: first, everyone is imperfect; second, no one can alter the past; and finally, each person is responsible for his or her own actions.

In Isaiah 58:1–12, the Lord demanded that the people of Israel reconcile their relationships with one another as a condition for enjoying an authentic relationship with Him. Because they had mistreated their brothers and sisters, their worship had become empty and hypocritical, though they believed themselves to be righteous. To help His people recover their original, authentic zeal, the Lord gave them specific instructions to restore their relationships despite how badly they had blown it in the past.

To prepare for this lesson, read Isaiah 58:1–12 and chapter 10 in *Parenting: From Surviving to Thriving*.

Leader Help

By the end of this lesson, group members should recognize that their estranged relationships affect their relationship with the Lord, understand the five steps for restoring a broken relationship as found in Isaiah 58:1–12, and commit to reconciling with at least one person they have offended.

131

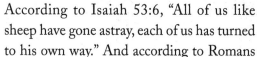

YOU ARE HERE

According to Isaiah 53:6, "All of us like sheep have gone astray, each of us has turned to his own way." And according to Romans 3:23, "all have sinned." So it's fair to assume that each of us has "blown it" with someone, which may have done great damage to our relationship with that person. Our offense may be a single incident or a repeated failure over a long period of time. It may be relatively minor by most standards or quite severe. Regardless, the issue will always stand between us and those we have offended until someone chooses to address it.

As you consider the questions below, think of someone with whom you've blown it. If possible, choose a close family member with whom your relationship is not what it should be and in which some (if not most) of the responsibility for the breach lies with you. The emotional climate doesn't have to be icy or hostile to qualify. In fact, your interaction may be very cordial. If, however, the relationship lacks closeness or warmth, reconciliation is worth pursuing.

 Describe how you are associated with this person and the current state of the relationship.

Leader Help

The questions in this section can surface strong emotions. Guilt feelings often produce extreme defensiveness or extreme remorse. Steer the discussion away from those who appear very defensive and allow the Holy Spirit to deal with them in His way and on His schedule. Focus instead on those who appear sorrowful and are willing to share. Encourage them to use the principles in this lesson to address any guilt feelings constructively.

How would you describe the relationship when it was at its best?

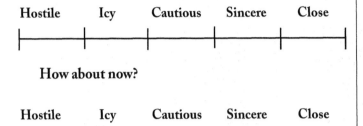

Hostile   Icy   Cautious   Sincere   Close

How about now?

Hostile   Icy   Cautious   Sincere   Close

What caused your relationship with this person to deteriorate?

What, if anything, have you done to attempt to restore the relationship? What effect did it have?

Fire may consume the wood, hay, and stubble of life, but the memories remain. That is, if you were careful to make them. Memories rarely make themselves.

—*Parenting: From Surviving to Thriving*

Despite how wrong the other person has been, either in causing the rift or perpetuating it, how have you been wrong? If you need additional perspective, ask your mate or a trusted friend—and be willing to listen without defending yourself.

DISCOVERING THE WAY

The people of Judah meticulously followed the rites and traditions of worship and felt sure their diligence pleased God. However, their pride had turned their hearts cold and hard. In this atmosphere of phony, self-centered religiosity, Isaiah brought a shocking message to his Hebrew brothers and sisters. The Lord was not pleased by their outward show of devotion in the temple because their conduct toward one another told a different story. In Isaiah 58:1–2, God gave His prophet a message to deliver.

Leader Help

For this section, we have elected to use the New English Translation of the Bible. This version faithfully reflects the original language while making the passage easier to comprehend. Group members can access this entire version of the Bible online at www.bible.org.

[1]"Shout loudly! Don't be quiet! Yell as loud as a trumpet! Confront my people with their rebellious deeds; confront Jacob's family with their sin! [2]They seek me day after day; they want to know my requirements, like a nation that does what is right and does not reject the law of their God. They ask me for just decrees; they want to be near God. [3]They lament, 'Why don't you notice when we fast? Why don't you pay attention when we humble ourselves?' Look, at the same time you fast, you satisfy your selfish desires, you oppress your workers. [4]Look, your fasting is accompanied by arguments, brawls, and fist fights. Do not fast as you do today, trying to make your voice heard in heaven." (Isaiah 58:1–4 NET)

In verse 1, the Lord declared that His people continued to commit rebellious deeds. What, according to verse 4, was their sin?

In verse 2, God affirmed that His people sought Him with the boldness of a righteous nation. According to verse 3, how had they tried to get the Lord's attention?

Based on verses 3–4, why had their religious activities failed to get them what they desired?

⁵"Is this really the kind of fasting I want? Do I want a day when people just humble themselves, bowing their heads like a reed and stretching out on sackcloth and ashes? Is this really what you call a fast, a day that is pleasing to the Lord? ⁶No, this is the kind of fast I want. I want you to remove the sinful chains, to tear away the ropes of the burdensome yoke, to set free the oppressed, and to break every burdensome yoke. ⁷I want you to share your food with the hungry and to provide shelter for homeless, oppressed people. When you see someone naked, clothe him! Don't turn your back on your own flesh and blood!" (Isaiah 58:5–7 NET)

According to God's thinking, a right relationship with Him will naturally result in a genuine love for others. . . . The Lord declared that His people had blown it by mistreating one another. They allowed wrong things to remain unresolved and to grow, destroying their relationships in the process. As a result, their worship was tainted with hypocrisy.

—*Parenting: From Surviving to Thriving*

We are selfish, proud, stubborn creatures who do our best to figure out life as best we can and, in the process, establish destructive habits that work well for us. And because they work, we feel sure they must be right, despite the pain we cause others along the way.

—*Parenting: From Surviving to Thriving*

In verse 5, the Lord described what many would consider a genuine, sacrificial attempt to hear from Him and gain His blessing. What, according to verse 6, did He truly want from His people?

Before the advent of machine power, farmers used animals to pull their plows and power their mills. To bind an ox or a mule to its task, a woodworker custom-carved a beam to fit across the shoulders of the animal. Lines of rope or leather ran from this "yoke" to the equipment the beast was to pull.

For obvious reasons, the yoke became a metaphor for any kind of severe servitude, grueling labor, or inescapable subjection (see Leviticus 26:13; 1 Kings 12:4; Jeremiah 28:2; 30:8; Lamentations 1:14; Acts 15:10). In the case addressed by Isaiah 58:6, one Hebrew had figuratively placed a yoke on the shoulders of another Hebrew, reducing him or her to the level of an animal.

8 "Then your light will shine like the sunrise; your restoration will quickly arrive; your godly behavior will go before you, and the Lord's splendor will be your rear guard. 9Then you will call out, and the Lord will respond; you will cry out, and he will reply, 'Here I am.' You must remove the burdensome yoke from among you and stop pointing fingers and speaking sinfully. 10You must actively help the hungry and feed the oppressed. Then your light will dispel the darkness, and your dark-

ness will be transformed into noonday. [11]The Lord will continually lead you; he will feed you even in parched regions. He will give you renewed strength, and you will be like a well-watered garden, like a spring that continually produces water. [12]Your perpetual ruins will be rebuilt; you will reestablish the ancient foundations. You will be called, 'The one who repairs broken walls, the one who makes the streets livable again.'" (Isaiah 58:8–12 NET)

According to Isaiah 58:9, what does the yoke represent?

GETTING TO THE ROOT

"Stop pointing fingers and speaking sinfully." (Isaiah 58:9 NET)

The Hebrew word translated "sinfully" in Isaiah 58:9 has a wide range of meanings depending on the context. It can mean "toil," "iniquity," or "deception," and in this passage, all three interpretations may help to flesh out our understanding of the Lord's accusation against the Hebrew people. The *Theological Wordbook of the Old Testament* adds the comment, "Generally, biblical theologians have given little attention to [this term] as a contributor to an understanding of sin. Since the word stresses the planning and expression of deception and points to the painful aftermath of sin, it should be noted more."[1]

In the context of the ancient world, "pointing the finger was involved in a formal accusation (as in Hammurabi's laws). The omen literature attaches to the gesture the power of a curse. [In Isaiah 58:9], it is indicative of malevolent slander."[2] In this case, it is possible that wealthier Hebrews "spoke sinfully," that is deceptively, against their brothers and sisters in the courts in order to take control of their land and reduce them to indentured servanthood. (See also Nehemiah 5:1–5.)

 Based on your study of Isaiah 58:6–10, how was a Hebrew to "break the yoke" in practical terms?

 Circle the word "then" in Isaiah 58:10. It marks an important transition in the passage.

Based on 58:10–12, describe in your own words how life would be different for the people of Judah if they were to obey the Lord.

Dr. Jeffrey Bingham, Professor of Theological Studies at Dallas Theological Seminary, illustrated the importance of maintaining healthy relationships by pointing out that when a man marries a woman who has children by a previous marriage, his vows are not to her alone. A man can't possibly love the woman without also loving the people she made.[3]

The same concept is true in our relationship with the Lord and with His children. He declared that His people had blown it by mistreating one another. Moreover, they had allowed their offenses to remain unresolved and to grow, destroying their relationships in the process. As a result, their relationship with the Lord continued to deteriorate. If they refused to reconcile with their brothers and sisters, they would also forfeit the wealth of blessings the Lord desired to give them.

STARTING YOUR JOURNEY

The Lord's instructions to the people of Judah in Isaiah 58:1–12 illustrate five steps we can follow as we seek to restore a broken relationship. As we consider and act on them, we must keep three unpleasant realities in mind. They may seem obvious, but they will help us hold realistic expectations and allow the other person the freedom to respond authentically.

First, *every person on earth is imperfect.* Our unwillingness to accept the imperfections of others (and of ourselves) keeps us stewing in our resentment, which shuts down any desire for reconciliation. When we ignore the simple fact that misunderstandings, hurt feelings, and selfishness are the norm, our expectations get out of whack; we lose our capacity for compassion. Our actions must be guided by love, grace, and humility.

Second, *no person can change the past.* Accepting that

the past cannot be altered will help us focus where we can have an impact: the future.

Third, *each person is personally responsible for his or her own issues.* We can't fix another person, nor can we motivate him or her to change. We can only evaluate ourselves and focus on how we can choose wisely regardless of how others behave.

Five Steps Toward Reconciliation After You've Blown It

1. *Humble yourself.*

In Isaiah 58:7–8, the Lord wanted those who had oppressed others to free them from their yoke and supply any needs that came about as a result of their offenses. In the New Testament, Jesus equated service to the very least of society as an expression of true humility.

Take a few moments to read the following passages. When you choose to humble yourself, to whom are you ultimately submitting?

> Psalm 138:6
> Matthew 20:24–28
> Matthew 23:12
> Luke 9:46–48 (see also Mark 9:33–37)
> 1 Peter 5:5

The restoration process must begin with a humble heart and a willingness to admit fault, accompanied by a genuine concern for the good of the other person above our own needs or desires.

Leader Help

The following questions are intended for individual reflection. As you discuss each step, allow group members sufficient time to think and respond privately before moving to the next.

Thinking of the person you recalled at the beginning of this lesson, how much empathy or compassion do you have for him or her?

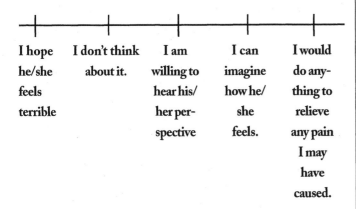

| I hope he/she feels terrible | I don't think about it. | I am willing to hear his/her perspective | I can imagine how he/she feels. | I would do anything to relieve any pain I may have caused. |

Why do you think you feel this way?

What do you suppose would soften your heart if you don't already have compassion for the person you offended?

2. Pray.

In Isaiah 58:3, the people cried out, "Why have we fasted and You do not see? Why have we humbled ourselves and You do not notice?" In reply, the Lord declared that their prayers had no effect because they were self-centered and oppressive—two sure signs that empathy, compassion, and humility were missing.

In Isaiah 58:9, the Lord encouraged the worship of the people once they had humbled themselves, and He delighted to answer their requests once they were offered with pure hearts. Humble prayers declare our dependence upon the Lord and usually involve the concerns of others over self.

Before attempting to reconcile any relationship, we must pray. Our prayer might look like the following:

Lord, I feel awkward. I have erected so many barriers between us, and he/she has built a number of his/her own. Time has only deepened the hurt. I want to restore this relationship, but without Your help, Lord, my timing will be wrong and I won't use the right words. So I call upon You to help me discern the right time and form the best words. Help me to heal the harm I have done.

Take a few moments to write a brief prayer for the person you offended and ask the Lord to lead you through the process of reconciliation.

> As for humility, the Lord isn't impressed by our ability to go without food. To Him, humility is regarding others as more important than self. And as long as we're not preoccupied with taking care of ourselves, we leave Him room to do it for us.
>
> —*Parenting: From Surviving to Thriving*

3. *Remove the yoke.*

In Isaiah 58:9, the "yoke" involved pointing an accusatory finger and speaking evil. The restoration process depends upon removing that yoke from our loved one. Before we approach the person we have offended, we must drop the accusations. We must prepare ourselves by refusing to lay any blame. The other person may indeed own a lot of the responsibility for the strained relationship, but that is a matter for the Lord to resolve. Removing the yoke of blame and shame from the shoulders of the other will free us up to start on the next step.

What fault have you been attributing to the person with whom you are estranged? What do you think he or she has done to contribute to the current state of your relationship?

Are you willing to forgive the wrongs he or she has done? ❑ Yes ❑ No

If so, then fill in the appropriate spaces below and read your commitment aloud, preferably to someone who will help hold you accountable.

I, _____, on this day,
_____ choose to forgive

*_____ for the offenses
I described above. I will no longer hold this against
him or her. I do not expect him or her to apologize or
otherwise make it up to me, but I will graciously accept
anything he or she chooses to offer. I will not revisit the
offenses with others, including the person who harmed
me. I realize that only the grace of Jesus Christ will
heal my wounded spirit and relieve my resentment. I
accept that this may be a gradual process that may take
a long time. Nevertheless, whenever I feel the need to
rehash the wrongs done to me, I will take them to the
Lord in prayer and ask Him to heal me.*

If the wounds you suffered are particularly deep, you
may find it helpful to make a copy of this commitment
and keep it in your wallet or purse. Whenever you are
tempted to resume the blame game, remind yourself of
the day you chose to forgive. Then express your frustration to the Lord. In time, as you heal, you will find less
and less need to pray about the particular matter or to
remind yourself of the choice you made on this day.

4. *Make yourself available and vulnerable.*
In Isaiah 58:10–11, the Lord required His people to
go beyond removing the yoke; He also expected them to
give expression to their humility by meeting the deepest
needs of the people they had harmed. If a broken relationship is to be restored, we must make ourselves vulnerable enough to acknowledge our wrong and to accept the
consequences. This is best done in person. And for the
apology to be genuine, we must at least be willing to give
the person we offended an opportunity to take his or her
justice, if the person needs that.

Envision yourself in a conversation with the offended person. Suppose you fully acknowledge your fault in causing the relationship to fail or to remain unhealed and the other person responds with angry, hurtful words. How do you react?

How might your willingness to listen, empathize, and respond with sincere sorrow affect the other person?

5. *Consider yourself a restorer.*

Not all relationships can be restored. Sometimes people prefer to hold on to their resentment, allowing righteous indignation to justify their distance. So our very best efforts may not be enough to repair the breach. Nevertheless, the Lord will honor our obedience. When we consider ourselves a "restorer," our heart and attitude change to wanting what's best for the other person and for the relationship. That may take a variety of forms. Our relationship with the other person may never be as close as it once was—in some cases, it may not be healthy to be. But in others, making the effort to reconcile will open the doors for a more intimate, vibrant relationship.

In Isaiah 58:11–12, the Lord didn't promise that the once-oppressed people would respond with forgiveness, gratitude, and grace. In fact, He said nothing about their response. However, He did promise that the once-guilty people would experience a renewed relationship with Him and that the Promised Land would become a lush, green, well-watered oasis—a testament to the humble, gracious character of the people and their God.

Regardless of whether we are able to restore that broken relationship, we can legitimately consider ourselves "restorers," or repairers of the breach, because we have obeyed God by lifting the yoke of oppression. We will have been transformed, and the abundance of our lives will reflect the well-watered intimacy we enjoy with the Lord.

Lesson Eleven

When God's Gift Comes Specially Wrapped

— Isaiah 45:5–10; Psalm 139:13–16; John 9:1–3;
Exodus 4:10–12; Romans 11:33–36 —

THE HEART OF THE MATTER

Perhaps nothing challenges our confidence in the sovereignty and goodness of God more than seeing a child with disabilities. Despite how this might agitate our personal sensibilities, the Lord does allow children to be born with missing limbs, contorted bodies, or damaged brains. Contrary to our fears, disabilities are not God's judgment for sin. In fact, Scripture teaches that the Lord ordains a sacred purpose for them. As with all weaknesses, disabilities provide Him an opportunity to display His grace and glory.

However the world might view people with disabilities, they are God's prized creations, "fearfully and wonderfully made" to bear His image with dignity and joy. His plan includes their unique contributions, which have no less importance than those of anyone else.

To prepare for this lesson, read Isaiah 45:5–10; Psalm 139:13–16; John 9:1–3; Exodus 4:10–12; Romans 11:33–36; and chapter 11 in *Parenting: From Surviving to Thriving*.

Leader Help

By the end of this lesson, group members should understand the relationship between God's sovereignty and the presence of pain in the world, take comfort in His sovereignty, and appreciate the unique contributions of people with special needs. They should also commit to reaching out to people with disabilities instead of withdrawing.

147

YOU ARE HERE

For centuries, atheistic philosophers have offered an argument against the existence of God that many call "the problem of evil" or "the problem of pain." They claim that a good god has the *desire* to eliminate evil, and an all-powerful god has the *ability* to eliminate evil. Because evil persists in the world, they conclude that God cannot be both good *and* all-powerful, which would therefore mean that the God of the Bible does not exist.

The argument does little to persuade believers, but many find it unsettling, especially when they encounter a child with disabilities.

Suppose you and your spouse are expecting a child. You receive a report from the doctor that your unborn child has a condition called *anencephaly*. The neural tube has failed to close, so the fetus has developed only a rudimentary brain stem—with little or no brain at all. Your baby will be born blind, deaf, and unconscious, and he or she will survive only a few hours or a number of weeks without life support. How would this affect your understanding of God?

Which would you tend to doubt first: God's goodness or His power? Why?

Psalm 139:14 declares that humans are "fearfully and wonderfully made." Does this description apply to the baby described above? Why or why not?

What personal experiences do you have with people who have physical or mental challenges or disabilities?

What effect do you think this person's disability has on God's plan in the world?

With the Lord, no diagnosis comes as a surprise, although we might be shocked. And with the Lord, there are no unexpected children or unwanted pregnancies. God never looks on a child as a mistake, nor does He regard any of them unfit, undesirable, substandard, or "defective."

—*Parenting: From Surviving to Thriving*

DISCOVERING THE WAY

The problem of evil continues to be a problem only when one doubts or rejects the sovereignty of God, which includes His sole right to define what is good and what is evil. When we accuse God of being unfair, we presume to judge Him by our own standards, which is laughable when we consider our qualifications to judge. And when we try to prove the goodness of God to ourselves or to others, we again presume to reconcile His acts to our standard of right and wrong.

The Lord is omnipotent (all-powerful), omniscient (all-knowing), and omnipresent (existing everywhere at once). It's a hard truth to accept at times, but our feeble, limited, selfish perspective affords us no grounds to doubt or reject His sovereignty or goodness. Rather than try to prove His goodness, we must, as a matter of faith, choose to accept the holy, righteous, blameless character of God as our foundation and reconcile the world to it.

Taking God's Sovereignty Personally

The Lord is sovereign over all. Nothing occurs in the universe except by His permission, including evil. Scripture is filled with expressions of God's sovereignty. For example, in Isaiah 45, the Lord claimed His right to rule His universe His way. In a speech recorded by Isaiah, one of His prophets, the Lord announced His plans to empower the pagan Medo-Persian king Cyrus to invade and conquer Babylon, which had taken the Israelites captive. Later, Cyrus would allow the Jews to return to the Promised Land and even assist them with rebuilding—all according to the Lord's orchestration of world events.

Read Isaiah 45:1–10 and "Getting to the Root," keeping in mind that neither the Medo-Persians nor the Babylonians recognized the Israelite God as sovereign. According to Isaiah 45:7, the Lord "brings about peace and creates calamity" (NET). How would the Medo-Persians, the Babylonians, and the Israelites each view these concepts differently, given their respective situations?

Leader Help

Daniel 5 records how the Medo-Persian armies captured Babylon. (Many scholars suggest that Darius was either another name for Cyrus or was Cyrus's vice-regent over the old capital of the empire.) The story of how Cyrus returned the exiled Jews to the Promised Land can be found in Ezra 1. If you believe that your group is unfamiliar with Jewish history, you may choose to summarize these chapters for them or read them aloud.

What impact does our perspective have on how we define peace and calamity?

"One who argues with his creator is in great danger, one who is like a mere shard among the other shards on the ground! The clay should not say to the potter, 'What in the world are you doing? Your work lacks skill!' Danger awaits one who says to his father, 'What in the world are you fathering?' and to his mother, 'What in the world are you bringing forth?'" (Isaiah 45:9–10 NET)

 Isaiah 45:9–10 uses three analogies to help us understand the nature of God's sovereignty. What are they?

In your own words, summarize what you know about the concept of God's sovereignty. How does your understanding of this concept affect your perspective when you see a child with disabilities?

Special-needs children do impact the world, and their parents have a much more important job than they realize. Their children challenge our most basic system of values—those beliefs that shape our understanding of human esteem, worth, and acceptance. Each encounter with a disabled or mentally challenged child becomes a crisis of principles because they remind us that the kingdom of God looks at people from a very different perspective.

—Parenting: From Surviving to Thriving

GETTING TO THE ROOT

According to Isaiah 45:7, the Lord "forms light and creates darkness," "brings about peace and creates calamity" (NET). This passage uses a literary device scholars call *merism*, a means of illustrating totality by highlighting its contrasting parts. We might say, "John looked high and low" to emphasize that he looked everywhere.

Light and darkness are opposites, just like the Hebrew words *shalom* and *rah*, translated "peace" and "calamity." *Shalom* includes the ideas of prosperity, completeness, soundness, safety, health, satisfaction, and friendship. As we have seen, to bid someone *shalom* is to wish upon them the greatest possible state of well-being. *Rah* can mean a number of things, such as evil, distress, misery, or adversity, depending upon the context. In this setting, it refers to the very opposite of *shalom*.

According to Isaiah 45:7, the Lord sovereignly presides over both. Speaking through the prophet, He declared that He exercises absolute dominion over everything, even so far as moving the world's greatest political and military powers like pawns in order to accomplish His will. In order to accomplish His plan to bring *shalom* (peace) to Israel, He was about to bring *rah* (calamity) upon Babylon.

The Hebrew word God used in Isaiah 45:9 when He said, "Woe to the one who quarrels with His *Maker*" is the same root word translated as "ordained" in Psalm 139:16. God "made" the days of those who are disabled from birth long before they were conceived.

Psalm 139 praises God for His sovereign care and design and was written to be sung in the first person by the worshiper. Before reading Psalm 139:13–16, think of a particular child you know who has special needs. Then, as you read the passage, use your imagination to hear the child speaking the words. Try to experience the psalm from his or her perspective.

 Read Psalm 139:13–16. How might this psalm be a comfort to someone disabled from birth?

How might it make him or her angry?

Biblical Answers to Difficult Questions

Even for someone who affirms and accepts God's sovereignty, doubts can be troublesome, especially when they are founded in legitimate questions. When we encounter children born with physical or mental disabilities, three troubling questions in particular tend to surface. Scripture provides the perspective we need to deal wisely with these sensitive issues.

1. *Did someone's sin cause the child's disability or abnormality?*

Jesus faced this question when He and His disciples happened upon a man born blind.

Most new moms and dads dream of rearing the next Einstein, Mozart, or the next sports phenomenon, and when their little one shows early signs of mental disability, they might be tempted to think that their job is somehow less important. Profoundly disabled little boys and girls aren't likely to change the world on a grand scale. However, like you and me, they do impact their part of it.

—Parenting: From Surviving to Thriving

Read about this encounter in John 9:1–3. Who does Jesus say caused the blindness?

In John 9:3, what reason does Jesus give for the man's affliction?

Though a few Jewish sects in Jesus's day believed that a fetus could be guilty of sin, most Jews believed birth defects were God's retribution for the sin of the parents. As soon as Jesus finished correcting the theology of His disciples, He declared, "I am the Light of the world" and gave the man sight (John 9:5–7). In this one act of mercy, Jesus demonstrated His authority over disabilities, sin, bad theology, the temple, the Sabbath, and even the very Pharisees who opposed Him (John 9:1–41). He was afforded this opportunity because a little baby came into the world without the ability to see. God did not cause the baby's affliction; He gave it divine purpose before anything had been created.

2. *How is God involved in birth defects and disabilities?*
We know from our study so far that the Lord is absolutely sovereign, yet He does not cause bad things to occur, such as physical and mental disabilities. However, they do occur by His permission and He does ordain their purpose within His plan. Remember Isaiah 45:5–10?

Cyrus chose to invade Babylon to satisfy his own selfish ambition. The Lord *allowed* Cyrus to proceed and used his lust for power to accomplish His own plan.

A congenital defect may afflict a child as a result of being born into a fallen world, but the Lord will always use that misfortune to accomplish His purposes. In Exodus 3:10, God ordered Moses to lead His people out of Egypt. Moses had spent the previous forty years tending sheep in exile because he had tried to free the Hebrews using his own leadership skills, training, and initiative—his own strength. Having failed miserably, Moses now offered one reason after another to convince the Lord that he was the wrong man for the job. Finally, he offered what he believed to be an insurmountable obstacle: his disability.

 Read Exodus 4:10–12. According to verse 10, what was Moses's disability?

Why would this disability reduce Moses's likelihood of success?

What was God's response to the very real complication introduced by Moses's disability? What was His solution?

Forty years earlier, Moses failed to free the Hebrews when he acted on his own initiative and abilities (see Exodus 2:11–15). How did his disability ultimately become the key to his success?

Because the Lord is sovereign, He gives divine purpose even to the very qualities individuals like least about themselves, including physical or mental challenges. In doing so, He includes each of us in His plan, even making disabilities a central part of its success.

3. *Why does God wait to put an end to evil? Why does He not do it now?*

Unfortunately, the answer to this question is, "No one knows." Even if we were able to answer this question to complete satisfaction, another question would take its place, causing no less confusion or doubt. Paul, near the end of his great theological treatise to the Romans, acknowledged that many of the Lord's ways remain a mystery. Rather than succumbing to doubt and despair over it, he praised God, uttering the words,

Oh, the depth of the riches both of the wisdom and knowledge of God! How unsearchable are His judgments and unfathomable His ways! For who has known the mind of the Lord, or who became His counselor? Or who has first given to Him that it might be paid back to him again? For from Him and through Him and to Him are all things. To Him be the glory forever. Amen. (Romans 11:33–36)

At some point, even the most brilliant and accomplished theological minds must choose to trust God's character in the absence of tidy resolutions. For those who choose to accept His sovereignty, the problem of evil poses very little threat.

STARTING YOUR JOURNEY

The purpose of theology is to shape our thinking according to the truth of Scripture so that our behavior will reflect the Lord's character. When Jesus encountered the man born blind in John 9, He used the opportunity to straighten out the disciples' twisted theology. Then He took action.

This should be our model. The truth of Scripture should transform our thinking, and our actions should reflect the new insights we gain.

If a person genuinely believes that a disabled child was uniquely crafted by God to fulfill His purposes, describe how his or her behavior will reflect this truth in the following situations:

- An autistic child becomes completely absorbed in a book of maps and refuses to interact with other children.

Leader Help

As part of your preparation, consider asking the parents of the disabled child you featured in the lesson to suggest what treatment the child would most appreciate from others. You might even invite the parents to join your meeting at this point.

- A child in a wheelchair watches as other children at a petting zoo enjoy playing with the animals in the pen.

- A friend becomes despondent because a prenatal exam reveals that his or her baby has Down syndrome.

- A blind woman at a party sits alone, contentedly listening to the roomful of sounds.

- A children's hospital in your area needs volunteers.

≈

What we believe about God determines how we live our lives. Our theology affects everything about us: our decisions, how we will react to the circumstances of life, even how we will behave toward one another.

—*Parenting: From Surviving to Thriving*

≈

The Lord does not offer any justification to prove His goodness; however, He did give us sufficient reason to accept it. Twenty centuries ago, the almighty, sovereign God of the universe made the problem of evil His own by becoming one of us in the person of Jesus Christ. If we are truly His disciples, we will see His creation as He sees it and be moved to compassion as Jesus was. We can move beyond questioning the sovereignty or goodness of God so that we might become the means of His grace to those with disabilities—His beloved, specially wrapped gifts to the world.

Lesson Twelve

Final Words to Families Then and Now

— Deuteronomy 6:1–24 —

THE HEART OF THE MATTER

In Deuteronomy 6, Israel stood on the threshold of the Promised Land for the second time. The first generation after the exodus had failed to enter the land forty years earlier because they feared their enemies more than they feared the Lord. Moses wanted to be sure that this new generation would not fail to claim the blessings God had waiting for them, so he reiterated the Lord's statutes, this time with the encouragement, "for our good always and for our survival" (Deuteronomy 6:24). This preamble to Moses's final series of messages to Israel provides no fewer than six applicable principles that sustained families four thousand years ago and can strengthen ours today.

To prepare for this lesson, read Deuteronomy 6:1–24 and chapter 12 in *Parenting: From Surviving to Thriving*.

YOU ARE HERE

Books on parenting do a good business, especially among two important groups: parents of rebellious or struggling children and new parents hoping to avoid the fate of the first group. While the

Leader Help

By the end of this lesson, group members should recognize the necessity of a relationship with the Lord and of His Word to the health and survival of the family and the crucial role of the family in teaching each new generation about Him. They should also commit themselves to cultivating a love for the Lord in their homes and to living in authentic dependence upon Him.

Leader Help

To underscore this point, do some research at a popular online bookseller. Enter the search term "parenting," and note the number of books available for purchase. At the time of this workbook's publication, a popular online bookseller offered 3,558 different titles on the subject of parenting.

advice of seasoned childrearing experts can certainly help, nothing surpasses the value of a home saturated with love for God and characterized by an authentic desire to know and apply His Word.

 How "real" is God in your home? In what ways is your faith evident in your everyday conversations and interactions within the household?

In what ways does Scripture fit into the rhythm and routine of your household?

If all your family knew about God came by watching your relationship with Him—how you make decisions, recover from failure, or handle disappointments—what kind of God would they see?

Describe a time when you felt particularly close to the Lord. What was occurring in your life at the time? What spiritual disciplines were you practicing at the time (e.g., prayer, Bible reading, journaling)?

 ## DISCOVERING THE WAY

The people of Israel stood near the banks of the Jordan River, poised to enter the land God had promised them for centuries. But deadly pagan influences permeated the land flowing with milk and honey. Before God's chosen people entered a brand-new phase of existence as a nation, Moses wanted to be sure they understood how to survive the threats they would face.

As you read Deuteronomy 6:1–24, use your imagination. Picture yourself in the modern-day equivalent of their position: You recently landed a huge promotion at ten times your old salary and with a benefits package like you've never dreamed. Last weekend, you and your family toured your new house, a prime piece of real estate, the dwelling of your grandest fantasy. Your children's education, your retirement, and a biannual luxury vacation for the next twenty years are virtually guaranteed. And best of all, your new prosperity came to you as a gift from God. What will be the blessings of living this new way of life? What will be the risks?

Moses's address to families then and now contains no fewer than six principles by which to live. If we heed

Leader Help
The example of newfound prosperity may not resonate with the members of your group. Ask them to describe their version of sudden financial blessing and encourage them to explore the possible dangers to their spiritual life if this dream were to come true.

them, we can survive the dangers that prosperity can bring.

GETTING TO THE ROOT

For millennia, Jews have held Deuteronomy 6:4 as the quintessential declaration of their faith, a pledge of allegiance to the one and only true God. The passage continues on to describe the only appropriate response to this theological declaration: love. Real, authentic love. They call it the "Shema" because the passage begins with the Hebrew command: "Hear!" "Listen!" "Don't miss this!" Upon rising every morning and just before going to bed, faithful Jews will recite the Shema: "Hear, O Israel! The LORD is our God, the LORD is one! You shall love the LORD your God with all your heart and with all your soul and with all your might. These words, which I am commanding you today, shall be on your heart" (Deuteronomy 6:4–6).

Principle 1 (Deuteronomy 6:4–7)

We should note that this command was, and is, issued to heads of households. Not to government officials, not to religious leaders, but to *parents*.

Read Deuteronomy 6:4–7. According to 6:7, what are parents supposed to do with the Lord's words?

We can choose to forget Him, forsake His commandments, ignore His warnings, and allow our prosperity and pagan influences to woo us away from dependence upon the Lord, but we do so at our own peril. Those He has called, He has saved; and He will preserve those He has saved to the end. However, He has given us a large stake in determining the quality of our own lives and those of the little people He has given us to steward. He has given us the power to shape the environment in which we rear our children and to choose the legacy we pass on to them.

—*Parenting: From Surviving to Thriving*

Can a parent effectively accomplish the command of verse 7 before that of verse 6? Why or why not?

The repeated words of Deuteronomy 6:5 should remind us that parents must personally develop a rich, authentic relationship with the Lord before they can influence their children in a godly, healthy way.

So, the first principle of Deuteronomy 6:1–24 is this: *Parents cannot pass along what they themselves do not possess.*

Principle 2 (Deuteronomy 6:7)

The phrase "diligently teach" in Deuteronomy 6:7 comes from the Hebrew word *shanan*, meaning "to sharpen."[1] Moses used it to paint a vivid word picture of someone scraping a whetstone across a blade over and over again until the edge is razor sharp. A dramatic and accurate translation would be, "You shall intensely sharpen your sons with these words."

Eugene Peterson's paraphrase reads, "Get [these words] inside your children. Talk about them wherever you are, sitting at home or walking in the street; talk about them from the time you get up in the morning to when you fall into bed at night" (Deuteronomy 6:7 MSG).

 Where should teaching about the Lord take place, according to Deuteronomy 6:7?

Kids are ruthlessly practical. They want to know what works. They don't want to waste their time believing in something that doesn't make sense or won't have a significant impact on their lives. And if they see you giving the Lord the scraps of your time, your money, and your energy, what are they to conclude? Only that love for the Lord can be discarded without consequence.

—*Parenting: From Surviving to Thriving*

What benefit(s) does the child gain from this approach?

Suppose a child's parents were to faithfully take him or her to church each Sunday but never participate personally. What are some assumptions the child might make?

How would this practice affect the child's relationship with God and his or her spiritual development?

Children have an insatiable appetite for practical learning. With all of the information coming to their eyes and ears, they want to know what works and what doesn't. And they observe their parents in order to make the distinction. The beliefs we live by become the lessons they learn.

The second principle: *Children won't benefit from what isn't authentic.*

Principle 3 (Deuteronomy 6:8–9)

The command of the Lord didn't stop at the threshold of the home. The Shema wasn't intended to be simply repeated; it was to be lived. These words were to be a public declaration as well as a private commitment.

 Read Deuteronomy 6:8–9. Why do you think the Lord wanted His people to be so public about their beliefs?

In what area of your life is it most difficult or uncomfortable to act on or declare God's truth? Why?

How does our courage to stand for truth in public contribute to the spiritual development of our children? Be specific.

Take authenticity out of Christianity, and all you have is religion. All knowledge, no wisdom. Ritual without heart. Nothing of any practical value for facing challenges that ruin lives. The challenges we face don't come in the form of multiple-choice Bible quizzes. They test our character. They prove the genuineness of our belief, the reality of our relationship with God. And our children are watching.

—*Parenting: From Surviving to Thriving*

Most of us want to be liked more than we want to be right. This is especially true when we must face the competing values of our society during those times when we're cut off from the support of our Christian friends and relatives. As difficult as these situations can be, they tend to clarify our genuine beliefs—for ourselves as well as our children.

The third principle: *Truth isn't a core commitment if it lacks courageous convictions.*

Principle 4 (Deuteronomy 6:10–12)

Next, Moses revealed the source of his concern for the Israelites entering the Promised Land.

 Read Deuteronomy 6:10–12. What four specific blessings were the Hebrew people about to receive?

What had the Israelites done to earn those blessings?

What, according to verse 12, did Moses fear would happen as a result of such overwhelming, unearned affluence?

God described the land they were about to settle in as one "flowing with milk and honey" (Deuteronomy 6:3).

Abundance. Prosperity. Affluence. Wealth can be both a blessing and a trial. The land of Canaan possessed all the goodness that God wanted to grant His chosen, beloved people. But it also involved contact with spiritually corrupt people who were given to astounding brutality, sexual perversion, and pagan worship. The temptation to neglect or reject the God who had provided for them would be fierce.

The fourth principle found in Moses's admonition is this: *Getting much without personal sacrifice often leads to indifference toward God.*

Principle 5 (Deuteronomy 6:13–17)

The Lord didn't command the Israelites to burn the orchards, scorch the land, and reduce the cities to rubble. He wanted His covenant people to enjoy everything the land of plenty had to offer. And in His grace, He gave it to them—they didn't have to earn it for themselves. However, He did make some demands for their good and for their survival.

> 13"You shall fear only the LORD your God; and you shall worship Him and swear by His name. 14You shall not follow other gods, any of the gods of the peoples who surround you, 15for the LORD your God in the midst of you is a jealous God; otherwise the anger of the LORD your God will be kindled against you, and He will wipe you off the face of the earth. 16You shall not put the LORD your God to the test, as you tested Him at Massah. 17You should diligently keep the commandments of the LORD your God, and His testimonies and His statutes which He has commanded you."
> (Deuteronomy 6:13–17)

Children bypass what we say and even what we *think* we believe, and they zero in on what our *actions* say we believe.

—*Parenting: From Surviving to Thriving*

According to Deuteronomy 6:13–17, what specific commands did the Lord give the Israelites?

"You shall _____" (6:13).

"You shall _____" (6:13).

"You should _____" (6:17).

What did the Lord specifically forbid the Israelites from doing?

"You shall not _____" (6:14).

"You shall not _____" (6:16).

What would be the Israelites' greatest temptation to abandon the Lord? (see Deuteronomy 6:14).

Why is this temptation so powerful? Does it exist in our culture today? What does it look like?

The surrounding nations would present a tantalizing alternative to trusting only the Lord. They enjoyed great abundance while worshiping false gods, readily adopting the worship of any deity that promised to fulfill their desires. Today, we would call them "tolerant."

So we can state the fifth principle as *Compromising faith in the one true God is politically correct but spiritually lethal.*

Principle 6 (Deuteronomy 6:18–24)

In Deuteronomy 6:18–24, the Lord turned His focus back to the importance of teaching in the family.

 Read Deuteronomy 6:18–24. When a child asks about the purpose of God's commands, what story was the Israelite supposed to tell? (see 6:21–23).

What two reasons are given to the child in 6:24 to explain why the Israelites were to obey the Lord's commandments?

Let's face it; most of us want to be liked more than we want to be upright. . . . Speaking up might label you as someone who's not a team player. Those moments of truth tend to clarify one's core commitments. Genuine core commitments don't crumble under pressure. In fact, they usually grow stronger.

—*Parenting: From Surviving to Thriving*

The Lord brought His chosen people out of slavery in order to give them mind-boggling abundance by His grace. This should tell us that God's exclusive standards and stern warnings served to preserve the freedom and happiness of His people, not to keep them in bondage and misery.

The sixth and final principle: *Mercy brought us out; grace brings us in; obedience enables us to survive.*

Thousands of years after the Exodus from Egypt, Jewish families today still gather to celebrate God's faithfulness to them with a feast. This very special night involves an intricate, fifteen-step ritual meal that involves everyone in the family, from the elderly to the young.

Traditionally, the youngest member of the family is to ask four questions during the feast, to which the older generations respond. Here are the questions and typical answers:

Question 1: "Why is it that on all other nights during the year we eat either bread or matzoh (bread without yeast), but on this night we eat only matzoh?"
Answer: "We eat only matzoh because our ancestors could not wait for their breads to rise when they were fleeing slavery in Egypt, and so they baked the dough while it was still flat, which was matzoh."

Question 2: "Why is it that on all other nights we eat all kinds of herbs, but on this night we eat only bitter herbs?"
Answer: "We eat only moror, a bitter herb, to remind us of the bitterness of slavery that our ancestors endured while in Egypt."

Question 3: "Why is it that on all other nights we do not dip our herbs even once, but on this night we dip them twice?"
Answer: "We dip twice—first, green vegetables (or parsley) in salt water; and, second, moror in charoset, a sweet mixture of nuts and wine. The

first dip, green vegetables in salt water, symbolizes the replacing of tears with gratefulness, and the second dip, moror in charoset, symbolizes sweetening the burden of bitterness and suffering to lessen its pain."

Question 4: "Why is it that on all other nights we eat while sitting, but on this night we eat in a reclining position?"
Answer: "We recline at the table because in ancient times, a person who reclined at a meal symbolized a free person, free from slavery, and so we recline to remind ourselves of the glory of freedom."

Throughout the Old Testament and on into today, the children of Israel look to the exodus as proof of God's goodness and faithfulness. In the retelling of the story, they renew their hope and, in the process, new generations learn about the might and mercy of God. (For more information on Passover, see Exodus 12.)

Look at the commands the Lord gave Israelite families that were coping with the stresses of affluence and competing religions: Watch out! Remember! Obey! Teach! Do this for your good and for your survival. The six principles found in Deuteronomy 6:1–24 point to one overarching theme, one essential message:

Prepare the next generation for unexpected trials by living in authentic dependence upon the almighty, omniscient Creator of the universe.

The Lord didn't call us to change the world, only to be faithful. What happens after we live and proclaim the truth is His responsibility.
—*Parenting: From Surviving to Thriving*

STARTING YOUR JOURNEY

As parents given the responsibility for the spiritual development of our children, we can learn to live in authentic dependence on the Lord by maintaining three interconnected priorities in the following order: love and obey our Lord, take good care of our families, and live peacefully with others. Let's take a closer look at each one.

1. *Love and obey our Lord.*

Good parenting begins by maintaining close, personal intimacy with the Lord. We cannot possibly pass on to our children what we ourselves do not possess. When we enjoy closeness with God, we are better equipped to lead our children as we model authenticity, and perhaps most important, we maintain a soft heart.

When do you regularly spend time alone reading and reflecting on God's Word each week?

When do you contribute your God-given abilities to those who need help or to extending Christ's kingdom?

Leader Help

The questions in this section are not marked as primary questions because they are intensely personal and intended for individuals to complete on their own. They are essential to the teaching goals of this lesson, so please allow group members adequate time to complete these questions within the session or assign them as homework.

Where do you regularly join with other Christians in worshiping God?

How do you feel about your prayer life, generally speaking?

Developing a personal relationship with God can sound mysterious or even hyper-religious, but the Lord has made spiritual growth remarkably accessible to everyone. To find out how to begin a relationship with God through Jesus Christ, see page 177. If you would like to learn how to love and obey the Lord with greater depth and consistency, we highly recommend that you read Charles R. Swindoll, *So, You Want to Be Like Christ? Eight Essentials to Get You There* (Nashville: W Publishing Group, 2004). This book will simplify and demystify eight spiritual activities in very practical and relevant terms so that even busy working parents can grow closer to God and influence their children to do the same.

2. Take good care of our families.

Because physical needs tend to be more immediate and visible, few parents fail to provide adequate food, clothing, and shelter for their children. Emotional availability and adequate time for spiritual development, on the other hand, can easily take a backseat to a parent's career devel-

It's not enough that we know the truth; we must live the truth with courageous conviction for it to mean anything to others, including our children.

—*Parenting: From Surviving to Thriving*

opment and personal fulfillment. Deuteronomy 6:7 describes a parent spending many hours with his or her child talking about the Lord as they experience life together.

On average, how much time do you spend with your children each week?

~

Cynthia and I have delighted to give our four kids the best we could afford. We want them to enjoy our abundance before we're gone. But never at the expense of their relationship with the Lord. As you give to your children, help them cultivate a heart of thanksgiving. Always point them to the provision and protection of the Lord, the true source of all that's good.

—Parenting: From Surviving to Thriving

If you're not doing so already, what can you sacrifice in order to spend no fewer than eight hours per week with your children?

Bible stories are a wonderful way to teach our children about the Lord and how to love and obey Him. He gave your children *you* for the very same reason. Let them learn about God from the stories of your life. They will not only grow closer to Him, they'll grow closer to you as well.

Describe a time when you saw the unmistakable hand of God intervening to comfort, protect, or prosper you.

How do you think it would impact your children if you told them this story?

3. *Live peacefully with others.*

Our horizontal relationships with others reflect our vertical relationship with the Lord. As we have peace with God, we will discover that our relationships with others will grow strong and secure. Furthermore, our children see the authenticity of our relationship with God in how we treat others.

How well do you know your neighbors?

When is the last time you made life a little easier for a neighbor?

How can you and your children reach out to a least one neighbor to build a good rapport?

The Lord created the institution of the family for a very good reason. What better way to prepare the next generation for unexpected trials than by example? What better training could there be for children than watching their parents wrestle with change and grow in their relationships with God? The way to prepare the next generation for the trials of prosperity and competing loyalties is by living in authentic dependence upon the almighty, omniscient, Creator of the universe. As our children see us live out our faith and as they witness the Lord's faithful provision and protection, they will be more likely to love Him with all their hearts and with all their souls and with all their might.

How to Begin a Relationship with God

We have in our heavenly Father the perfect parent. And as parents ourselves, we can appreciate the deep, unrelenting love that He has for His children. We identify with the joy He experiences when His children live in harmony with their design and enjoy success. And we can empathize with His sorrow when His children choose disobedience or rebellion over intimacy with Him.

No relationship means as much as our bond with the Father, and our interaction with other people—including our children—can never be completely whole unless this primary relationship has been restored. The most marvelous book in the world, the Bible, tells us how we can know and enjoy our heavenly Father, explaining four vital truths. Let's look at each truth in detail.

OUR SPIRITUAL CONDITION: TOTALLY CORRUPT

The first truth is rather personal. One look in the mirror of Scripture, and our human condition becomes painfully clear:

> There is none righteous, not even one;
> There is none who understands,
> There is none who seeks for God;
> All have turned aside, together they have become useless;
> There is none who does good,
> There is not even one. (Romans 3:10–12)

We are all sinners through and through—totally corrupt. Now, that doesn't mean we've committed every atrocity known to humankind. We're not as *bad* as we can be, just as *bad off* as we can be. Sin colors all our thoughts, motives, words, and actions.

Look around. Everything around us bears the smudge marks of our sinful nature. Despite our best efforts to create a perfect world, crime statistics continue to soar, divorce rates keep climbing, and families keep crumbling.

Something has gone terribly wrong in our society and in ourselves, something deadly. Contrary to how the world would repackage it, me-first living doesn't equal rugged individuality and freedom; it equals death. As Paul said in his letter to the Romans, "The wages of sin is death" (Romans 6:23)—our emotional and physical death through sin's destructiveness, and our spiritual death from God's righteous judgment of our sin. This brings us to the second truth: God's character.

GOD'S CHARACTER: INFINITELY HOLY

Solomon observed the condition of the world and the people in it and concluded, "Vanity of vanities! All is vanity" (Ecclesiastes 1:2; 12:8). The fact that we know things are not as they should be points us to a standard of goodness beyond ourselves. Our sense of injustice in life on earth implies a perfect standard of justice elsewhere. That standard and source is God Himself. And God's standard of holiness contrasts starkly with our sinful condition.

Scripture says that "God is Light, and in Him there is no darkness at all" (1 John 1:5). He is absolutely holy—which creates a problem for us. If He is so pure, how can we who are so impure relate to Him?

Perhaps we could try being better people, try to tilt the balance in favor of our good deeds, or seek out wisdom and knowledge for self-improvement. Throughout history, people have attempted to live up to God's standard by keeping the Ten Commandments or living by their own code of ethics. Unfortunately, no one can come close to satisfying the demands of God's law (Romans 3:20). So, what can we do?

OUR NEED: A SUBSTITUTE

Here we are, sinners by nature, sinners by choice, trying to pull ourselves up by our own bootstraps and attain a relationship with our holy Creator. But every time we try, we fall flat on our faces. We can't live a good enough life to make up for our sin because God's standard isn't "good enough"—it's perfection. And we can't make amends for the offense our sin has created without dying for it.

Who can get us out of this mess?

If someone could live perfectly, honoring God's law, and would bear sin's death penalty for us—in our place—then we would be saved from our predicament. But is there such a person? Thankfully, yes!

Meet your substitute—*Jesus Christ*. He is the One who took death's place for you!

> [God] made [Jesus Christ] who knew no sin to be sin on our behalf, so that we might become the righteousness of God in Him. (2 Corinthians 5:21)

GOD'S PROVISION: A SAVIOR

God rescued us by sending His Son, Jesus, to die for our sins on the cross (1 John 4:9–10). Jesus was fully human and fully divine (John 1:1, 18), a truth that ensures His understanding of our weaknesses, His power to forgive, and His ability to bridge the gap between God and us (Romans 5:6–11). In short, we are "justified as a gift by His grace through the redemption which is in Christ Jesus" (Romans 3:24). Two words in this verse bear further explanation: *justified* and *redemption*.

Justification is God's act of mercy, in which He declares believing sinners righteous, while they are still in their sinning state. Justification doesn't mean that God *makes* us righteous, so that we never sin again, rather that He *declares* us righteous—much like a judge pardons a guilty criminal. Because Jesus took our sin upon Himself and suffered our judgment on the cross, God forgives our debt and proclaims us *pardoned*.

Redemption is God's act of paying the ransom price to release us from our bondage to sin. Held hostage by Satan, we were shackled by the iron chains of sin and death. But, like a loving parent whose child has been kidnapped, God willingly paid the ransom for you. And what a price He paid! He gave His only Son to bear our sins—past, present, and future. Jesus's death and resurrection broke our chains and set us free to become children of God (Romans 6:16–18, 22; Galatians 4:4–7).

OUR RESPONSE: FAITH IN CHRIST

These four truths describe how God has provided a way to Himself through Jesus Christ. Since the price has been paid in full by God, we must respond to His free gift of eternal life in total faith and confidence in Him to save us. We must step forward into the relationship with God that He has prepared for us—not by doing good works or being a good person but by coming to Him just as we are and accepting His justification and redemption by faith.

For by grace you have been saved through faith; and that not of yourselves, it is the gift of God; not as a result of works, so that no one may boast. (Ephesians 2:8–9)

We accept God's gift of salvation simply by placing our faith in Christ alone for the forgiveness of our sins. Would you like to enter a relationship with your Creator by trusting in Christ as your Savior? If so, here's a simple prayer you can use to express your faith:

Dear God,

I know that my sin has put a barrier between You and me. Thank You for sending Your Son, Jesus, to die in my place. I trust in Jesus alone to forgive my sins, and I accept His gift of eternal life. I ask Jesus to be my personal Savior and the Lord of my life. Thank You.

In Jesus's name, amen.

If you've prayed this prayer or one like it and you wish to find out more about knowing God and His plan for you, contact us at Insight for Living. You can speak to one of our pastors on staff by calling the number or writing to us at the address below.

Insight for Living
P.O. Box 269000
Plano, TX 75026-9000
1-800-772–8888

Notes

Unless otherwise noted, all material in this workbook is adapted from the *Parenting: From Surviving to Thriving* sermon series and companion book by Charles R. Swindoll and was supplemented by the Creative Ministries department of Insight for Living.

Lesson One: The Best-Kept Secret of Wise Parenting
1. Francis F. Brown, S. R. Driver, and Charles A. Briggs, *The Brown-Driver-Briggs Hebrew and English Lexicon* (Peabody, MA: Hendrickson, 2000), 335.
2. Ibid.
3. Ibid.

Lesson Two: Understanding How Your Child Was Made
1. Bruce L. Shelley, *Church History in Plain Language* (Waco, TX: Word, 1982), 145.
2. Robert A. Pyne, *Humanity & Sin: The Creation, Fall, and Redemption of Humanity* (Nashville: W Publishing Group, 1999), 174.

Lesson Three: Establishing a Life of Self-Control
1. W. E. Vine, Merrill F. Unger, and William White, *Vine's Complete Expository Dictionary of Old and New Testament Words*, vol. 1 (Nashville: Thomas Nelson, 1996), 164.
2. James Dobson, *The Strong-Willed Child: Birth Through Adolescence* (Wheaton, IL: Tyndale, 1978), 30.
3. Ibid., 32.

Lesson Four: Cultivating a Life of Self-Worth
1. William Barclay, *The Letters to the Galatians and Ephesians* (Philadelphia: Westminster, 1958), 211–12.
2. e. e. cummings, "A Poet's Advice," Ottowa Hills High School *Spectator* (26 October 1955), quoted in Charles Norman, *E. E. Cummings: The Magic Maker* (New York: Bobbs-Merrill, 1972), 353.
3. *Merriam-Webster's Collegiate Dictionary*, 10th ed., see "authenticity."

4.   James Strong, *The Exhaustive Concordance of the Bible* (Nashville: Abingdon, 1973), 54.

5.   Charles R. Swindoll, *Parenting: From Surviving to Thriving* (Nashville: W Publishing Group, 2006).

Lesson Five: Secret Struggles . . . Family Troubles

1.   *Merriam-Webster's Collegiate Dictionary*, 11th ed., s.v. "authentic."

2.   Eric Hoffer, *The Passionate State of Mind and Other Aphorisms* (New York: Harper & Row, 1955), 45.

3.   Ibid., 39.

4.   Tim Kimmel, *Why Christian Kids Rebel* (Nashville: W Publishing Group, a division of Thomas Nelson, Inc. 2004), 214. Used by permission of Thomas Nelson, Inc., Nashville, Tennessee. All rights reserved.

Lesson Six: From Resentment to Rebellion

1.   *Merriam-Webster's Collegiate Dictionary*, 11th ed., see "vulnerable."

Lesson Seven: Affirming and Encouraging Words to Parents

1.   *Merriam-Webster's Collegiate Dictionary*, 10th ed., see "prodigal."

2.   Gerhard Kittel, ed., *Theological Dictionary of the New Testament*, vol. 1 (Grand Rapids: Eerdmans, 1987), 507.

Lesson Eight: Confronting the "Older Brother Attitudes"

1.   Henri J. M. Nouwen, *The Return of the Prodigal Son: A Story of Homecoming* (New York: Doubleday, 1994), 70.

2.   Ibid.

3.   J. M. Wilson, "Birthright," in *The International Standard Bible Encyclopedia*, ed. Geoffrey W. Bromiley, vol. 1 (Grand Rapids: Eerdmans, 1979), 515–16.

4.   Eric Hoffer, *The Passionate State of Mind and Other Aphorisms* (New York: Harper & Row, 1955), 40.

Lesson Nine: Increasing the Priority of Your Family

1.   See Charles R. Swindoll, *Marriage: From Surviving to Thriving* (Nashville: W Publishing Group, 2006), 25.

2.   Alvin Toffler, *The Third Wave* (New York: Bantam, 1981), 28.

3.   Barbara Bush, "Remarks of Mrs. Bush at Wellesley College Commencement," http://www.wellesley.edu/PublicAffairs/Commencement/1990/bush.html, accessed 15 May 2006.

Lesson Ten: Restoring Relationships After You've Blown It

1.   R. Laird Harris, Gleason L. Archer, and Bruce K. Waltke, eds. *Theological Wordbook of the Old Testament*, vol. 1 (Chicago: Moody, 1980), 23.

2.   John H. Walton, Victor H. Matthews, and Mark W. Chavalas, *The IVP Bible Background Commentary: Old Testament* (Downers Grove, IL: InterVarsity, 2000), 638.

3.   Taken from a class lecture of Dr. Jeffrey Bingham, Professor of Theological Studies at Dallas Theological Seminary (April 2004) Used by permission.

Lesson Twelve: Final Words to Families Then and Now

1. Francis F. Brown, S. R. Driver, and C. A. Briggs, *A Hebrew and English Lexicon of the Old Testament with an Appendix Containing the Biblical Aramaic* (Oxford: Clarendon, n.d.), 1041.

Printed in the USA
CPSIA information can be obtained
at www.ICGtesting.com
LVHW080749050824
787165LV00006B/14